Made in His Image

*Overcoming Low Self-Esteem by
Discovering the Real You!*

Kenneth D. Phelps

xulon
PRESS

Copyright © 2002 by Kenneth D. Phelps

Made in His Image
by Kenneth D. Phelps
IMANI Faith Publishing/IMANI Faith Productions © ℗

Printed in the United States of America

Library of Congress Control Number: 2002111441
ISBN 1-591602-07-6

All rights reserved. No part of this book may be reproduced in any form without written permission from IMANI Faith Publishing/IMANI Faith Productions.

Unless otherwise indicated, the Scripture quotations contained herein are from the New Revised Standard Version Bible, copyright © 1989 by the Division of Christian Education of the National Council of the Churches of Christ in the U.S.A., and are used by permission. All rights reserved.

PO Box 239
Bloomingdale, IL 60108
Website: www.imanifaithproductions.com
Email: pimanifaith@cs.com
© 2002 by Kenneth Phelps

IMANI Faith Publishing/IMANI Faith Productions Inc. is a Christian-based recording, publishing, and music entertainment company.

IMANI is a family of Christian entertainers and writers that, in addition to recording, also writes plays, books, and ministers at concerts, banquets, and special events.

IMANI is a place to showcase, market, and develop gifted Christian musical artists.

IMANI is an entertainment management and consulting organization. For more information, please visit our website at www.imanifaithproductions.com or write IMANI at PO Box 239, Bloomingdale, IL 60108. Telephone: 630-415-1900.

NOTE: This manuscript is the property of IMANI Faith Productions. Please do not duplicate or share with anyone without permission from IMANI or Kenneth D. Phelps.

Xulon Press
11350 Random Hills Road
Suite 800
Fairfax, VA 22030
(703) 279-6511
XulonPress.com

To order additional copies, call 1-866-909-BOOK (2665).

Contents

∞

Dedication vii
Acknowledgments ix
Preface/Introduction xi
Chapter I   Genesis 19
Chapter II   Community 23
Chapter III   Definition of Self-Esteem 31
Chapter IV   Biblical Presence of Low
                 Self-Esteem 43
Chapter V   The Survey 53
Chapter VI   Transformed Esteem—The Rebirth of
                 the Real You 57
Chapter VII   Self-Esteem and Ministry 65
Chapter VIII   Stages of Transformation 77
Chapter IX   Forgiveness: The Doorway to
                 Healing 85
The Final Chapter X:
                 It's Not Over—It's Just Beginning! 93
Bibliography 101
About the Author 103
About IMANI Faith Productions 105
IMANI Order Form 107
Appendix A 109

Dedication

This being my first book, I owe so much to so many, but I owe it all to Thee!

To God, who made me in His image and likeness: thank You. I dedicate this book to You.

To the love of my life, my wife, Veneeta B. Phelps—here we go again. I know that sometimes I may seem insane to you, but thank you for believing in me and supporting the IMANI vision unconditionally. I dedicate this book to you.

To my children, Kenneth, Morgan, and David, you all are my pride and joy. I love each of you with my whole heart. Each of you are unique and special in your own way. I dedicate this book to you.

To my pastors and their wives, the late Rev. James and Gladys Fair, the late Rev. Dr. U. Hughey, and Rev. Dr. M.E. and Louise Saunders, thank you for your godly example and embracing me as your son. I owe so much to you for the seed of ministry and the unconditional love you placed in me. I dedicate this book to you.

To all my mentors, teachers, and coaches, both good and bad, thank you for sharing your gifts and inspiring me to become a disciple. Special thanks to Dr. Bob Price at

NTBS for planting the seed of writing and publishing in the first place. This book is dedicated to you.

To Uncle Willie (Laura), Aunt RoRo (Casanova), Aunt Vivian (James), Aunt Donna, Gwen (Virgil), and Joyce (Johnnie), thank you for being a friend to Mama and for still loving me. Please don't be "trippin'" over the order in which your names are listed—I really do love you all equally. This book is dedicated to you.

To Granny, Dora Sanders, and Grandma Harris and the rest of my family and friends, thank you for being there. Especially my dad, Kenneth W. Phelps—I love you very much, not for what you were, but for who you are and, more importantly, what you are becoming. To ALL of my godchildren, this book is dedicated to you.

To my other father, mother, and sister, Dan, Annie, and Virginia Brewster, thank you so much for everything. I am forever in your debt! To Pastor Michael F. Mack and the Jerriel Baptist Church family, this book is dedicated to you.

To the greatest church in the world! The Concord Missionary Baptist Church in Chicago, Illinois—you all are the greatest. Thank you for your support down through the years. This book is dedicated to you.

To my Mother, the late Mary Marzette, the one who gave me life and who believed in me, even when I didn't believe in myself, this book is dedicated to you.

Finally, this book is dedicated to all those nameless individuals who feel they are forgotten or left out. This book is dedicated to you, too.

To God be the Glory!

—Kenneth

Acknowledgments

∞

    I could not have completed this work without the inspiration of the Holy Spirit and the aid, assistance, and feedback of many great minds.

    I am so grateful to my wife Veneeta Phelps, Vivian and James Robinson, Rev. Dr. Bob Price, Rev. Dr. John Bollinger, Rev. Dr. Carla Waterman, Derek Felton, Joyce Dinkins, Rev. Dr. Michael Noble, Calvin Giddens, Patricia Robinson, Eloise Edmerson, Pastor Melvin Jones, Rev. Chip Hall, Jessica Hall, Darla Steele, Judith Watts, Sharron Downs, Katy Scott, and Rev. Rev. Dr. M.E. Saunders for your honest and candid feedback.

    I am indebted to my Executive Assistant, Dianna Coleman, for helping me put everything together.

    To my attorney, accountant, and friend Donald Montgomery and accountant and friend Rev. Stephen Holloway, thank you for your wise counsel and assistance.

    To my proofers/editors and publisher at Xulon Press, thank you for all your hard work and the professional publishing assistance that you give to independent aspiring artists like me. Thank you for helping make my dreams a reality.

    Finally to the staff at IMANI Faith Productions, Inc., you all are the greatest. Thank you for supporting this project.

    God's choicest blessings be upon each of you!

—Kenneth

Preface/Introduction

So God created humankind in his image,
in the image of God he created them;
male and female he created them.
(Genesis 1:27)

I praise you, for I am fearfully and wonderfully made.
(Psalm 139:14(a))

    The cover of the June 4, 2001, issue of *JET* magazine featured the hottest new teen heartthrob, Bow Wow. As I thumbed through the pages of *JET* attempting to get to the feature story about Bow Wow, I stumbled upon two very interesting articles. The first was about former New York Yankees' star outfielder Darryl Strawberry, and the other was about the New Orleans Saints' star running back Ricky Williams. The headlines read, "Strawberry Spared Prison; Sentenced to More Drug Treatment" and "Saints' Ricky Williams Diagnosed with Disorder; says 'I am extremely shy.'" So I continued to read about both of these highly public and visible star athletes. One was on a quick path to imprisonment and self-destruction, and the other was seemingly lost in a world all by himself.

I was particularly interested in the Williams story. You might remember that Williams had a stellar college career. He was a star running back for the University of Texas Longhorns and the 1998 Heisman Trophy winner. Now Ricky was a star running back in the NFL with the New Orleans Saints. The article suggested that Williams had a social anxiety disorder, which he self-diagnosed as "being very shy." This new revelation came about after a severe bout with depression and abnormal reclusive behavior, such as wearing his football helmet during interviews, curling up in a fetal position inside his locker, and distancing himself from his teammates.

The other article featured Darryl Strawberry. Darryl was an all-star outfielder with the New York Yankees until he marred his career by participating in self-destructive behavior: drug addiction and constant run-ins with the law.

As I read both articles, I asked myself how could both of these young African American megastars who seemed to have it all—fame, money, success, and popularity—be in such predicaments? Their abnormal and self-destructive behaviors were similar, if not identical, to many African American brothers and sisters in America. Both Darryl Strawberry and Ricky Williams have self esteem issues. Unfortunately, they are not alone. Only God knows how many are stricken with the dreadful and devastating condition. If it could happen to them, it could and surely does happen to anyone.

I am not a social psychologist or psychiatrist by vocation, but I know esteem issues when I see it. I can iden-

Preface/Introduction

tify esteem issues, but not because my undergraduate psychology classes, my seminary classes on pastoral care or counseling, or my CPE (Clinical Practical Experience) prepared me to do so. I know self esteem issues when I see it because it happened to me! My esteem issues did not manifest itself in me as it did in Darryl and Ricky, but nevertheless it did have its effect on my life. I'm talking from personal experience. For years, I too was a victim of LSE (Low Self Esteem). But God healed me. Therefore I am writing from the viewpoint of one who has had LSE and has been healed and delivered from it! **Made in His Image** is the product of my personal reflection on that whole experience.

For years, I wore a mask of confidence. Even to this day, when I share my testimony with my closest friends and loved ones, they are shocked to discover that I was a victim of LSE. When they looked at my lifestyle and behavior "on the surface," everything appeared okay. "On the surface," it appeared that everything that I attempted to achieve after college was a success. For fourteen years, I was a successful computer systems engineer with the world's leading information publisher. I had been in the gospel ministry, preaching and teaching the Word of God. For seven years, I have had the privilege of serving as the pastor of a growing ministry, the Concord Missionary Baptist Church. In 1998, my wife and I started IMANI Faith Productions. IMANI Faith Productions is responsible for establishing the careers of Gospel Artist Montage Phelon and Youth Fellowship and Stellar Award 1999 New Artist of the Year Nominee, NuWave. I also wrote and produced the hit stage play, **New Beginning**. I was able to do all of this while having a happy marriage (to Veneeta) and raising two wonderful children (Morgan and David). We had money in the bank and I drove a Mercedes-Benz. On top of that, we live in a house with a picket fence in the suburbs. The only thing missing was a dog!

So "on the surface," it looked like everything was wonderful with my life. People would often tell me how proud they were of me and of what I had become. But I was not proud of myself and was suffering from LSE. In fact, I didn't feel good about anything I had achieved or accomplished except the establishment of my family. On the inside I was self-critical and judgmental and felt that nothing I ever did was good enough. At first I thought it was a spirit of humility that came with my salvation or calling. I now know that it was a symptom of my LSE, called perfectionism. Perfectionism is defined here as a pervading thought or spirit that constantly tells you that nothing is ever good enough! It's a "could've, would've, and should've" mentality that plays out in self-defeating conversations and conveniently reminds you of your shortcomings! So I camouflaged my LSE and learned to master the art of looking successful without feeling successful.

Most people think that those who are successful are exempt from LSE. Wrong! LSE victimizes anyone who will embrace it. Many successful people in all walks of life have LSE, but have learned to cover it up and function as expected by others.

LSE was my constant traveling buddy until the Spirit opened my eyes, unmasked me, and allowed me to really see myself. For the first time in many years, I got to see the real me again—not the person that everyone else wanted to see, but the real me. I experienced what I call "the right reflection," which allowed me to see that I was fearfully and wonderfully made in God's image and likeness. Then I became healed, delivered, and set free. Praise God! I was blind but now I can see! Finally I was able to look in the mirror to see and embrace the real me. I no longer needed to define myself in terms of athletic accomplishments, academic achievement, profession/vocation, or sexual conquests! I no longer needed others to validate my ministry or me. It took me many years to learn the fact that God doesn't make junk, nor does He make mistakes! No one is perfect—we *all* make mistakes—but God did not make a mistake when He made you and me!

First Things First

There are some things that you should know before you continue reading. First of all, in my quest for understanding, I drew from the disciplines of sociology, psychology, philosophy, and theology. Therefore this work includes insights from these disciplines and insights drawn from artistic works, such as plays, poems, and songs about self-esteem. I also include several socio-psychological profiles of biblical characters who I believe suffered from LSE. But **Made in His Image** is not intended to be an academic textbook or research project. If it happens to find its way through the halls of academia, it would be much more than I hoped for. **Made in His Image** is intended to stimulate or provoke thought, reflection, and hopefully inspire dialogue.

Secondly, **Made in His Image** is not intended to be

a comprehensive autobiography, even though some of the material is autobiographical in nature. It is autobiographical only in that it is the product of my own reflections and personal experience with and victory over LSE.

Thirdly, I define Low Self-Esteem as a devaluation of oneself. I firmly believe that LSE is an evil demonic spirit that is intentionally designed to torment, control, enslave, and ultimately destroy not only the individual, but also the community. Therefore LSE has both individual and communal dimensions and implications.

I further believe that individuals who suffer from LSE are mirroring, reflecting, or living out only what their immediate community and those who influence them are projecting onto them. Therefore, the solution to low self-esteem is to change the individual's image of self! This is primarily done by the transformation of the individual's spiritual and mental self-image, concept, and perception. This is what Paul was referring to in Romans 12:2, when he says, "Do not be conformed to this world, but be transformed by the renewing of your minds, so you may discern what is the will of God—what is good and acceptable and perfect." This spiritual and mental transformation is primarily the work of the Holy Spirit and secondarily the work of the human will. God has already healed us, but we have to want to be healed. We have to seek the truth and resist becoming the projections of others. That truth is that we are all made in His image and likeness (see Genesis 1:27) and we are fearfully and wonderfully made (see Psalm 137:14). That is the only reflection, image, or projection that we should be living out. I now know that God did not want me to do or be all those things I became just to impress or please others.

But the good news is that God is able to look beyond the mask and see the real you, not based upon your sin (past, present, or future!), but according to His divine purpose and design. Hallelujah! Now that's grace in action!

In some parts of the book, I speak in terms of the communal nature of LSE especially as it relates to the African American community. I do so primarily because I believe that LSE has a communal or social dimension. I also do so because that's my background and experience. I am an African American preacher who was born and raised in an African American community and now serve in an African American ministry context. However, I have extensive experience and exposure to other cultures and communities. Let me go on record as saying that I know LSE is not limited to the African American community. In fact, LSE is no respecter of culture or ethnic origin. It will possess and slowly destroy anyone of any age, race, gender, or social and economic class. LSE will reside wherever it is welcomed and nurtured.

The effects of LSE are devastating for any community. In my lifetime I have had the opportunity to do some traveling. I have spent time in Native American reservations in the midwestern and southwestern states of America. I have visited communities in the Appalachian Mountains and in barrios of Mexico and the southwestern states. I have toured Asian American communities in Chicago, LA, San Francisco, and New York. So I have seen the devastating effects of extreme poverty, illiteracy, and presence of LSE in these communities.

I have also seen the presence of LSE in the African American community. I believe the African American community is plagued with an epidemic of LSE. Many of my brothers and sisters are victims of this institutional satanic attack (racism). The presence of drugs, violence, illiteracy, crime, self-destruction, and incarceration in our community is at an all-time high. I believe this is no accident, but is destruction by Satan's design. It is embedded in the very fabric of our American society. This is part of the consequences of institutionalized racism, which is also inherently evil and designed to destroy and exploit all minority communities.

LSE should not be in any community. To change this, America must undergo a radical transformation and come to the understanding that "we are one, and one are we." Luke was right when he proclaimed in Acts 17:26 that God "hath made of one blood all nations of men for to dwell on all the face of the earth, and hath determined the times before appointed, and the bounds of their habitation" (KJV).

Lastly, **Made in His Image** is an invitation to dialogue, reflection, and healing. It was written from this backdrop and viewpoint. It is my prayer that this book will be a blessing to all who read it. And if you suffer from LSE, I pray that you will accept my invitation to dialogue, reflection, and healing and encounter a Holy Ghost makeover that will allow you to embrace the truth that you are all fearfully and wonderfully made in His image!

CHAPTER 1

Genesis

∞

"In the beginning God created the heaven and the earth. And God said, Let us make man in our image, after our likeness: and let them have dominion over the fish of the sea, and over the fowl of the air, and over the cattle, and over all the earth, and over every creeping thing that creepeth upon the earth. So God created man in His own image, in the image of God created he him; male and female created he them. And God blessed them, and God said unto them, Be fruitful, and multiply, and replenish the earth, and subdue it: and have dominion over the fish of the sea, and over the fowl of the air, and over every living thing that moveth upon the earth" (Genesis 1:1, 26–28 KJV).

In the beginning God created you and me in His image and likeness, and He gave us dominion over all of His created order! What a wonderful and profound truth—the God of the universe created you and me in His image and empowered us for dominion. So why are there so many

Made in His Image

people with distorted images? Why are so many people limited by self-hatred and destruction and living beneath their privilege? Let me tell you that the problem is not with God! So the next logical question is, wherein lies the problem? It's with us. I have learned that many roads lead to the destination of LSE (Low Self-Esteem). But the origin of LSE is a corrupted seed or a gross distortion of the image called the "self." In other words, the real issue is a mask—false image or identity.

We know that our identities or self-images are developed in the early stages of life. Some even suggest that the self is formed in the mother's womb. That's why it is important for parents (notice I didn't just say mothers, but fathers too!) to read and talk to their babies in the womb. It is important for the baby (and parents too) to be acknowledged, touched, held, and loved. This interaction, this expression of intimacy, can and should be experienced as early as possible because it is an important part of character development and self-esteem of the unborn baby.

Although I was born to unwed parents who had their issues, my mother (Mary Merkerson), father (Kenneth W. Phelps), and extended family loved me from day one. I knew that they loved me because they consistently showed me. Being the firstborn son and grandson, I was showered with lots of love and affection. My mother and family made me feel as if I could accomplish anything. Every accomplishment in the early stages of my development was an occasion for celebrations. We celebrated my "first" steps and "first" words. We even celebrated the "first" time I went to the bathroom on my own! My grandmother loves to brag, to anyone who will listen, how I did everything early. She swears that my first word was "granny"! Even to this day, after all these years, Granny still reminds me, "You were such a smart baby!" In my family, "firsts" were always occasions for celebration. This was key and critical in my formation as a person. Oh, how I looked forward to an achievement simply for the accompanying celebration. I loved to hear my mother, aunts, or grandmother bragging on the phone about something I did. Positive affirmation from loved ones is very important to the development of one's self-esteem. In fact, consistent, positive affirmation is very important throughout a person's life. Today, my wife, family, friends, and church members satisfy this need for me. They are my biggest supporters. Honestly, I like to hear them comment on my accomplishments.

Although I like affirmation from others, and strongly encourage others to become affirmers, I also need to say that the affirmation of others is not the primary motive or goal for the work that I do. I caution the reader against putting too much stock into the affirmation or confirmation of others. Praise and compliments can be addictive to the receiver and very abusive by the giver. Compliments can be manipulative and are therefore subject to the character of the one offering the compliment. If affirmation and praise are your chief motivators for the work that you do, then whatever you get is your reward. I believe that is what Jesus was trying to convey to His disciples when He said in the sixth chapter of Matthew:

> Take heed that ye do not your alms before men, to be seen of them: otherwise ye have no reward of

your Father which is in heaven. Therefore when thou doest thine alms, do not sound a trumpet before thee, as the hypocrites do in the synagogues and in the streets, that they may have glory of men. Verily I say unto you, They have their reward. But when thou doest alms, let not thy left hand know what thy right hand doeth: That thine alms may be in secret: and thy Father which seeth in secret himself shall reward thee openly. And when thou prayest, thou shalt not be as the hypocrites are: for they love to pray standing in the synagogues and in the corners of the streets, that they may be seen of men. Verily I say unto you, They have their reward. But thou, when thou prayest, enter into thy closet, and when thou hast shut thy door, pray to thy Father which is in secret; and thy Father which seeth in secret shall reward thee openly. (Matthew 6:1–6 (KJV))

So although I like to hear it, I now know that it is not my chief motive for the work I do, and the Lord knows I do not need others to validate me! And you don't, either. You really do not need others to validate you. God has done that. God validated you before He formed you in your mother's womb, and before you were born He consecrated you! The goal in all that we do should be to please God, who made us in His image and likeness.

CHAPTER II

Community

So, with so much love and affirmation, how and where did I contract LSE in the first place? Simple: community! Dietrich Bonhoeffer said, "Life is lived out in community." We all have to leave the comforts of home and go into the community.

I grew up in the late 1960's and early '70's in Maywood, Illinois. Maywood is located just west of Chicago. During those days, all of America was preoccupied with the Civil Rights movement and the Vietnam War. Chicago was a hotbed for civil rights and revolution. At one time, even Dr. Martin Luther King Jr. made his home in Chicago. Maywood was the birthplace and home of NBA stars Jim Brewer and Glenn "Doc" Rivers, and slain Black Panther Fred Hampton. In spite of it all, Maywood was a closely knit, family-oriented community. In fact, the building I lived in and the one next door were populated with family members or "family-like" people, meaning there was a lot of love and support for me. This love and support gave me security during a very violent and turbulent time in our community and country.

Elementary School

My next experience with community came when I went to Irving Elementary School. School is where I got a real education. School is where I learned how ignorant I was. At home, I was "the man." At school, I was just an average and sometimes below-average student who in the estimation of students and teachers was nothing special—just average. The problem for me was that on the inside, I knew I was someone special. But on the outside, in comparison to and by others, I was just average and nothing special. So I had an internal image or reflection conflict going on within me. The battle was between who I thought I was versus what others perceived me to be. Eventually the others won the battle, and I became what others in the larger community perceived me to be.

At Irving Elementary School, most of the teachers and administrators, particularly the principal Mr. William Frayser and Vice Principal Dr. Kovalik, were very nurturing and caring. They were like surrogate parents to the students. So Irving was like a home away from home. In retrospect, even though some of my teachers and coaches were hard and firm, I responded very well to those who took a special interest in me. But for those teachers who were indifferent to me, I performed terribly in their classes and my grades reflected it. My mother would always say to me, "Little boy, those teachers got theirs (referring to education/diploma).

You are there not to be liked, but to get yours!" And what she failed to communicate with words was communicated loudly and clearly with the belt![1]

In school we were evaluated based upon how well we did on assignments and tests. Grades and percentages were associated with every task we were to complete. So the goal of education for me wasn't to gain knowledge or understanding to better our world and myself. The goal of education for me was to make good grades. Needless to say, I failed miserably.

I firmly believe school is supposed to be a place where we develop the character and minds of our most prized treasures, our youth. However, my experience with the school system, especially high school, helped to perpetuate my condition of LSE.

High School

High school was a very difficult time for me. It was in this period of my life that I first became painfully aware of my self-esteem issues. So it is fair to say that my high school experience played a major part in the formation of my LSE. During the late 1970's and early '80's, most teens' self-esteem was influenced by one or a combination of several of the following external factors: academics, athletic achievements, popularity, reputation, or sexual conquests.

My self-esteem took a serious beating in high school. Murphy's law was my credo: "Whatever could go wrong did." In my mind, I wasn't great at anything positive, so my grades suffered. Athletically, I peaked and then became ineligible to play, so I spent most of my sophomore and junior years trying to get my grades together so that I could participate in sports. My mother and I talked about it and she concluded that all I needed was a little help. She went out and got me a tutor and enrolled me in remedial reading at school. At first I was excited about getting the additional help until my friends found out I was in this class and that I had a tutor. They made fun of me. So I did not want to go, but I continued until I brought my grades back up.

By the time I got my grades under control, the coach had lost confidence in me and would not let me play. Although my family, friends, and I appealed to the coach, he still would not let me play. Unfortunately, his opinion of me tremendously affected my game, and again I became a reflection of my coach's image of me.

It was not until years later that I learned that failing a test or not starting in a game did not make me a failure in life. What makes one a failure in life is not to try in the first place. My Grandmother Merkerson used to always say, "Nothing beats a failure but a try." Grades are just units of measurement. They do not define who we are! They really don't even tell us how much we know or don't know. Our society relies on this system of evaluation. It's the bedrock of our competitive society. Believe it or not, although it is not perfect, it is probably the "best" system that we have. What needs to change is not the method of evaluation, but the importance, focus, or weight that we place on grades. We need to pool our collective minds and find a balanced approach to teaching and evaluation.

The best example I can think of was modeled by my retired language professor, Dr. Estella Horning. Dr. Horning taught Hebrew and Greek at the Bethany and Northern Baptist Theological Seminaries in Lombard, Illinois. In some seminaries, Greek and Hebrew courses are used to "weed out" students. So I was really apprehensive about taking the courses in the first place. But Dr. Horning made what is traditionally believed to be a very difficult and challenging subject course into something very informative and fun. The first day, Dr. Horning said to the class, "You will establish or determine your grade in this class. And you may retake the quizzes and tests as often as you like to get the grades that you want to get out of this course." Then she said, "I want each of you to get good grades, but what matters most to me is that you learn the material, that you learn to read and write Greek (or Hebrew). And I am willing to give as much help as you need!" That really blew my mind, because up until that point, I thought that the goal of education was the grade. Here was a teacher who was not only interested in grades, but in her students learning. She was even willing to sacrifice her time and talents to make it happen! Our class really responded to Dr. Horning's challenge and teaching method. By the end of the course, we were all able to read and translate the texts. So she had accomplished her goal of teaching the students, and we all felt pretty good about ourselves in the process. It was a lot of work, but she made it fun. But the interesting thing is that the average test scores for both her Greek and Hebrew classes was over eighty-five percent. Wow!

I guess what I am saying is that when evaluating a person, we need to consider more than just his/her academic record. We need to evaluate the total person: his/her character and his life.

We also need to find a better way to build the character and esteem of students. This is what is lacking in our system and society. We need more educators like Dr. Horning, who see themselves as partners in education with their students and who are willing to invest their time and talent into building the character and esteem of our youth. We need more schools like Irving who are in partnership with the families and communities for the betterment of the children. School is where we invest in our future. School must not be a highly sophisticated daycare facility where teachers are glorified babysitters. Therefore, we need to seriously consider our educational system and make changes where necessary.

To make matters worse, like all youth at that age, my hormones were out of control. So I fell in and out of love several times and my heart was broken often. So I decided that love was for the birds and became what was called in those days a "Player." Ironically, "playing" was the one thing I was good at. Playing gave me a sense of purpose, power, and popularity. So playing is what I pursued and perfected. My esteem was then measured by sexual conquests. As long as I was with the finest girl in the school, I was somebody. As long as I could have as many girls as I could handle, I was somebody. How sad! I thank God that I have long since been delivered from that mentality of defining myself by the number of sexual conquests.

I thank God for my wilderness experience in school, because it was there I learned the power of resilience. And although I was constantly falling down, I always got back up. What did not kill me helped me. It helped me to be the husband, father, son, and man of God that I am today. Instead of making me bitter, it made me better. And what Satan meant for evil, God used for my good. But it didn't end there.

NOTES

[1] This statement is not to be interpreted in any way as an admission of child abuse or a statement condoning child abuse. I view my mother's behavior as a form of discipline and an act of tough love. It was never my mother's intent to hurt me physically or emotionally, but only to love and correct me when I was wrong. This was consistent with her theology and upbringing. This wasn't the norm; it was the exception.

CHAPTER III

Definition of Self-Esteem
∞

Self-esteem is the value or worth that individuals assign to themselves. Dr. Jerry Aldridge, in his book entitled *Self-Esteem, Loving Yourself at Every Age,* defines self-esteem as "The feeling of self-worth and self regard."[2] He further suggests the following six characteristics that are helpful to our understanding of self-esteem:

- Characteristic One: Self-esteem is described across the life span.
- Characteristic Two: Self-esteem is explained as both general and specific. People have a general feeling of self-worth but also self-esteem in many specific areas.
- Characteristic Three: Self-esteem is considered a spiral. Each of us has individual themes that come around again and again. Our reaction to these themes influences our self-regard.

- Characteristic Four: Self-esteem is also described as group or cultural. We have individual self-esteem, and we participate in the collective, cultural, or national self-esteem.
- Characteristic Five: Self-esteem is discussed in relation to the dark side of life.
- Characteristic Six: Special situations are also considered. People with disabilities, those from culturally diverse backgrounds, and women are presented in terms of their needs for self-esteem.[3]

The components that influence or make up one's self-esteem are self-image, self-concept, and self-confidence. (See Graphic #1: Self-Esteem #1.)

Graphic #1
Self-Esteem #1

Self Image, Concept and Confidence

Self-image is how one sees oneself. "It refers to how we picture ourselves. It is the image of how we look in terms

Definition of Self-Esteem

of our physical selves."[4] Self-image is how we visualize ourselves. Our wardrobe (which includes body piercing and tattoos) is an extension of our self-image. There is a direct correlation between how we dress and how we see ourselves. I often teach that there is a spirituality associated with one's wardrobe, which directly influences one's self-esteem or emotional state. A depressed individual will often dress depressed. A depressed person may not have the energy to properly groom or care for them selves. And to get out of depression, often times an individual will go shopping for a new outfit or go and get their nails and hair done. Somehow or another, the new outfit or pampering, makes one feel better about themselves and their self-image.

Self-concept is what we think about ourselves. "It is the thinking part of the self. It is what (or more importantly who) we think we are. People can think of themselves as many different things."[5]

And finally, self-confidence is what we believe we can do. Self-confidence is the faith that we have the ability in ourselves to accomplish what we set our minds out to do. These three factors (one's self-image, concept and confidence) influence and contribute to how we feel about ourselves. Therefore, self-esteem can also be defined as how individuals feel about themselves.In their book entitled *Preaching for Black Self-Esteem*, authors Henry Mitchell and Emil M. Thomas clarify their definition of self-esteem. They write, "By self-esteem we refer to the evaluation, which the individual makes and customarily maintains with regard to [himself]: it expresses an attitude of approval or disapproval, and indicates the extent to which the individual

Made in His Image

believes [himself] to be capable, significant, and worthy."[6]

Self-esteem comes in three forms: high, medium, and low. High self-esteem happens when individuals place a high value on themselves. This is often associated with pride and confidence. Unfortunately, today many see pride and confidence in negative terms. But that is not always valid. Taking pride in one's work, family, or accomplishments is a good thing. Confidence in who you are or your abilities to perform is also necessary and is a positive thing. But, like everything else, pride and confidence can be perverted. Perverted pride becomes egotistical. Perverted confidence becomes arrogance, cockiness, and over-confidence. Whenever possible, demonic spirits will pervert the sense of self (worth, value) within individuals so they will naturally think more highly of themselves than they ought to think! (See Graphic 2: Self-Esteem Chart)

Graphic #2
Self-Esteem Chart

LEVEL	CHARACTERISTICS
HIGH	SELF CENTERED ARROGANT COCKY SELF CONFIDENT
MEDIUM	GOD CENTERED HUMBLE MEEK
LOW	DEGRADATION DEPRESSED PEOPLEPLEASERS SELF HATRED

Definition of Self-Esteem

On the other end of the esteem spectrum is low self-esteem. This happens when individuals place little or no value upon themselves. This is often associated with weakness and self-abasement. LSE is a "belittling" of oneself, a type of "grasshopper mentality" (see Numbers 13:33). Individuals who suffer from LSE are often depressed and abusive toward themselves and often accept abuse from others.

In the middle of the esteem spectrum is medium esteem, which is a healthy sense of self. It is a balanced view of self—not too high and not too low. I believe that this is the space on the spectrum that we should be aiming for. This is the esteem that I believe is consistent with that of the Christian faith. Romans 12:3 says, "For by the grace given to me I say to everyone among you not to think of yourself more highly than you out to think, but to think with sober judgment, each according to the measure of faith that God has assigned."

So where do we get our self-esteem? According to Aldridge, "Self-esteem is constructed from inside each person through interaction with others and their environment. Of the many things, which interact to direct our self-esteem, eight of them are extremely important. These include the influence of 1) others, 2) institutions, 3) personalities, 4) experience, 5) history, 6) environments and social class, 7) our cultural heritage and 8) our decisions."[7] (See Graphic #3.)

Graphic #3
Esteem Influences

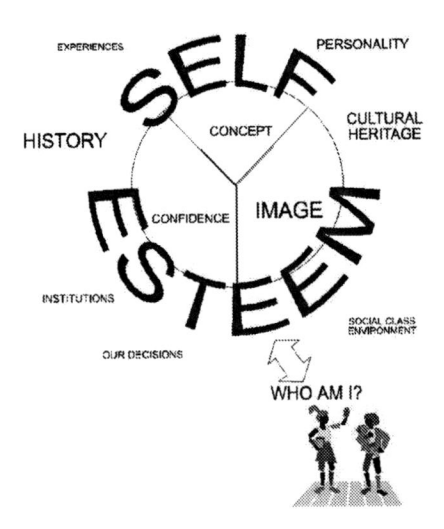

Diagram: "SELF ESTEEM" surrounding a circle divided into CONCEPT, CONFIDENCE, and IMAGE. Surrounding labels: EXPERIENCES, PERSONALITY, HISTORY, CULTURAL HERITAGE, INSTITUTIONS, SOCIAL CLASS ENVIRONMENT, OUR DECISIONS. Below: "WHO AM I?"

Behavioral scientist Abraham Maslow is noted for developing a hierarchy of motivational needs, including both physiological and psychological ones. Maslow believed these needs motivate human behavior. The seven levels/layers are:

1. Physiological: hunger, thirst, sex, etc.;
2. Safety/security;
3. Belongingness and love: affiliation with others, to be accepted;
4. Validation and esteem: to achieve, to be competent, to gain approval and recognition;
5. Cognitive: to know, understand, and explore;
6. Aesthetic: beauty, symmetry, and order;
7. Transcendence: to help others find self-fulfillment and realization of their potential.

Definition of Self-Esteem

Self esteem is formulated at level 3/4 – on Maslow's hierarcy of Human Needs.

(See Graphic #4. Maslow's Hierarchy of Human Needs.)

Graphic #4
Hierarchy of Human Needs

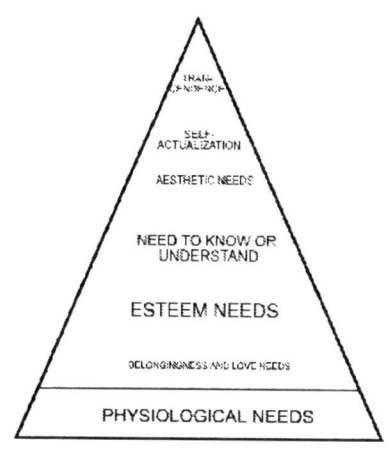

```
              /\
             /TRAN-\
            /SCEND-NCE\
           /   SELF-    \
          / ACTUALIZATION \
         /  AESTHETIC NEEDS  \
        /                      \
       /   NEED TO KNOW OR      \
      /       UNDERSTAND         \
     /                            \
    /        ESTEEM NEEDS          \
   /                                \
  /  BELONGINGNESS AND LOVE NEEDS    \
 /                                    \
/        PHYSIOLOGICAL NEEDS           \
----------------------------------------
```

I believe that in addition to these needs there are often social, spiritual, and communal needs that also influence human behavior and directly affect self-esteem.

Most people desire a sense of purpose, affirmation, popularity, love, success, and spirituality. This is similar to what Maslow is talking about, but I think where we part is the nature of human needs. I view human needs as cyclical rather than hierarchical. I think that human needs are driven in a cyclical fashion, depending on the perceived importance of that moment. (See Graphic 5: Cyclical Nature of Human Needs.)

Graphic #5
Cyclical Nature of Human Needs

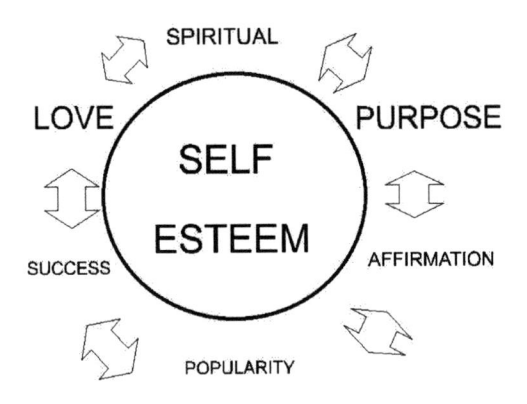

```
              SPIRITUAL
      LOVE              PURPOSE
            ┌─────────┐
            │  SELF   │
            │ ESTEEM  │
            └─────────┘
     SUCCESS           AFFIRMATION
              POPULARITY
```

By purpose, I mean that most people need to be a part of or doing something that is significant and that matters. I also mean knowing and being involved in one's life work. In the religious community, we call this one's calling or vocation. By affirmation, I simply mean to be affirmed in what we do and who we are. By popularity, we not only want to be praised for what we do, but we also want others to know who we are and what we do. We need love. Three Greek words are translated into the English word for love: *eros, philia,* and *agape. Eros* is a Greek word for a romantic type of love or intimacy, a relationship with someone to care for and to care about you. *Philia* is a Greek word for friendship, relationship, and fellowship. Agape is a Greek word conveying the "Godly" type of love. Agape is an unconditional and never-ending type of love. Agape is a type of love that loves the recipient in spite of their nature or character. The Apostle Paul defines the character and characteristics of this love in the thirteenth chapter of First Corinthians. By success, I am referring to our own evaluation of who we are and what we do relative to others who are doing the same type of work. Finally, by spirituality I am referring to the need to connect with a greater power outside of oneself. Spirituality is our inward drive to communicate with the divine. It is usually prompted or awakened by a life or communal crisis event. The most recent communal event to awaken the spiritual consciousness of America was the destruction of the World Trade Center towers in New York City and a wing of the Pentagon in Washington, D.C., by terrorists on September 11, 2001. Ever since that day, many Americans have been seeking encounters with the divine. Churches, mosques, temples, synagogues, and other places of worship are now filled to capacity. Even businesses and other institutions are trying to communicate with the divine—it is not uncommon to see business marquees and advertisements pleading with God to bless America.

I argue that the two greatest factors that influence self-esteem, especially today in America, are others and institutions. Particularly in the African American community, individuals place great importance and value upon the opinion, approval, and acceptance of others such as family, friends, and gangs, and institutions such as schools, community centers, faith communities (including churches, mosques, temples, etc.), and social organizations. One's "rep" (slang for reputation) is important and worth defending. To establish or to upgrade one's reputation, one must prove oneself. This acceptance or rejection helps to shape and mold one's self-esteem.

Media and Self Esteem

Also included in the "other" category for influencing our self-esteem, is the media. The media is a very powerful medium to communicate ideas, values, social norms and mores. Media defines and shape popular culture and directly influences one's self-image, concept and esteem. The media informs of society what is fashionable and therefore defines for us, what is hot, beautiful and sexy or not. When an individual compares them selves to what is on TV or in a video, it can be very discouraging and depressing.

Once our self-image and self-esteem are established, it is very hard to change. For example, it is now been more than twenty years since I graduated from high school and attended Wartburg College in Waverly, Iowa. Even now when I see my old school mates, they are shocked beyond belief when I tell them that I am a pastor of a church. They still see me in terms of what I was in school. My kids now go to school in the same community where I grew up, and my wife is a teacher in the same district where I went to school. Every now and then, I see people who "knew me when." After twenty years, my reputation still precedes me. But the good news is that in Christ I am a new creation; old things are passed away, and all things become new! (2 Corinthians 5:17.) That means that I have a new walk, a new talk, and a new reputation. The past no longer has dominion over me! It is not just for me. But it is also for you! We have new identities that are rooted and grounded in Christ!

NOTES

[2] Jerry Aldridge, Jr., *Self-Esteem: Loving Yourself at Every Age* (Birmingham: Doxa Books, 1993), 20.

[3] Ibid., 13.

[4] Ibid., 19.

[5] Ibid., 20.

[6] Henry H. Mitchell and Emil M Thomas, *Preaching for Black Self-Esteem* (Nashville: Abingdon Press, 1994), 26.

[7] Jerry Aldridge, Jr., *Self-Esteem: Loving Yourself at Every Age* (Birmingham: Doxa Books, 1993), 33.

CHAPTER IV

Biblical Presence of Low Self-Esteem

∞

Jesus was often confronted with individuals who suffered from LSE. One of the most intriguing is the encounter with the demoniac at Gerasene. Tradition has it that:

> They came to the other side of the sea, to the country of the Gerasenes. And when he had stepped out of the boat, immediately a man out of the tombs with an unclean spirit met him. He lived among the tombs; and no one could restrain him any more, even with a chain; for he had often been restrained with shackles and chains, but the chains he wrenched apart, and the shackles he broke in pieces; and no one had the strength to subdue him. Night and day among the tombs and on the mountains he was always howling and bruising himself with stones.

When he saw Jesus from a distance, he ran and bowed down before him; and he shouted at the top of his voice, "What have you to do with me, Jesus, Son of the Most High God? I adjure you by God, do not torment me." For he had said to him, "Come out of the man, you unclean spirit!" Then Jesus asked him, "What is your name?" He replied, "My name is Legion; for we are many." He begged him earnestly not to send them out of the country.

Now there on the hillside a great herd of swine was feeding; and the unclean spirits begged him, "Send us into the swine; let us enter them." So he gave them permission. And the unclean spirits came out and entered the swine; and the herd, numbering about two thousand, rushed down the steep bank into the sea, and were drowned in the sea.

The swineherds ran off and told it in the city and in the country. Then people came to see what it was that had happened. They came to Jesus and saw the demoniac sitting there, clothed and in his right mind, the very man who had had the legion; and they were afraid. Those who had seen what had happened to the demoniac and to the swine reported it. Then they began to beg Jesus to leave their neighborhood.

As he was getting into the boat, the man who had been possessed by demons begged him that he might be with him. But Jesus refused, and said to him, "Go home to your friends, and tell them how much the Lord has done for you, and what mercy he has shown you." And he went away and began to proclaim in the Decapolis how much Jesus had done for him; and everyone was amazed. (Mark 5:1–20)

Here we have Mark's account of a man who was demon possessed and was involved in self-destructive behavior. No doubt this man was the victim of institutionalized demonization. His condition made him unemployable and a social outcast; the only place he could find comfort, peace, and acceptance was in the graveyard! Everyone in the community knew this demoniac. They tried to contain and control him with fetters and chains, but they could not. And since they did not know what to do with him, they decided to incarcerate him in the graveyard. In the minids of the dominate culture incarceration was and still is less expensive and more cost-effective than rehabilitation!

In his book entitled *Unmasking the Powers,* Walter Wink advances the social context of the demoniac. He contends along with Rene Girard, "Human societies cannot face their own violence, nor can they permit endless retaliation against those who do express it." In other words, the community used the demoniac as a scapegoat; he was a reflection of their own violence and their demons. Wink suggests that the community not only ostracized the demoniac, but they also fed and kept it (him) alive, because it was in their best interest. This man was a reflection of their evil side. "The townspeople needed him to act out their own violence."[8]

Also in the text we see the dramatic transformation of the individual and the beginning of a communal transformation. This happens when Jesus casts out the demons and the man is restored back to his rightful place in his family and among the very community that projected their image upon him and enslaved him in the first place!

On another occasion, as Jesus was teaching in the synagogue, He was confronted by a woman and some men who suffered from LSE. John records in his gospel:

> Jesus went to the Mount of Olives. Early in the morning he came again to the temple. All the people came to him and he sat down and began to teach them. The scribes and the Pharisees brought a woman who had been caught in adultery; and making her stand before all of them, they said to him, "Teacher, this woman was caught in the very act of committing adultery. Now in the law Moses commanded us to stone such women. Now what do you say?" They said this to test him, so that they might have some charge to bring against him. Jesus bent down and wrote with his finger on the ground. When they kept on questioning him, he straightened up and said to them, "Let anyone among you who is without sin be the first to throw a stone at her." And once again he bent down and wrote on the ground. When they heard it, they went away, one by one, beginning with the elders; and Jesus was left alone with the woman standing before him. Jesus straightened up and said to her,

"Woman, where are they? Has no one condemned you?" She said, "No one, sir." And Jesus said, "Neither do I condemn you. Go your way, and from now on do not sin again." (John 8:1–11)

From the text, we see a community of men who I feel had esteem issues, because they were trying to make themselves look big by making this woman and Jesus look small. Individuals with LSE and inferiority complexes often attempt to make themselves look bigger by making others look smaller. These men violated this woman, first by participating in adulterous activities with her and then by publicly shaming and embarrassing her by bringing her before Jesus in the temple while He was in the midst of teaching. Their charge was adultery. The penalty according to the Mosaic Law was the death of both parties who violated the law (Leviticus 20:10, Deuteronomy 23:23–24). But only the woman was exposed and placed on trial. The men, like most individuals with LSE, hide behind the mask of self-righteousness and never expose their participation in the whole ordeal. Again, here we have a community of men (those in power and authority) who did not respect this woman (nor themselves) and a woman who accepted their projection of her. She felt powerless and allowed others to abuse her. It is very similar to that of a very promiscuous woman in the community who establishes her social status, or "rep," by losing respect for herself. The interesting thing about this text is this woman was so broken that she could not even defend herself. Therefore Jesus had to defend and heal her. Jesus restores her sense of self and repairs her self-esteem and simply says, "Woman, where are they? Has no one condemned you?" She said, "No one, sir." And Jesus said, "Neither do I condemn you. Go and do not sin again!" Her self-esteem was restored by the words of the master.

In both cases, we see the miraculous healing of LSE that can come only with a personal encounter with Jesus. The good news of the gospel is free to all, no matter our social, psychological, economic, gender, or racial/ethnic status. Romans 10:12–13 declares: "For there is no difference between the Jew and the Greek: for the same Lord over all is rich unto all that call upon him. For whosoever shall call upon the name of the Lord shall be saved" (KJV).

The next person who was tempted or tested by self-esteem issues I believe might surprise you. According to the Bible, "He was in the world, and the world was made by him, and the world knew him not. He came unto his own, and his own received him not" (John 1:10–11 KJV). This person was despised and rejected. He went to His own and His own people didn't receive Him. His friends were the lowlifes of the community. He befriended sinners and publicans. He even predicted His death by saying to His closest friends: "Behold, we go up to Jerusalem; and the Son of man shall be betrayed unto the chief priests and unto the scribes, and they shall condemn him to death, And shall deliver him to the Gentiles to mock, and to scourge, and to crucify him: and the third day he shall rise again" (Matthew 20:18–19 KJV). Shortly thereafter, He was falsely accused, beaten, spit on, and hung on an old rugged cross. While on the cross, He felt abandoned by His God. In agony, He cried, "My God, my God, why hast thou forsaken me?" (Matthew

27:46 KJV). And just before He died, He said, "It is finished." What is finished? The work of salvation that only Calvary and such a sacrifice could accomplish.

I think Isaiah says it best:

> He is despised and rejected of men; a man of sorrows, and acquainted with grief: and we hid as it were our faces from him; he was despised, and we esteemed him not.
>
> Surely he hath borne our griefs, and carried our sorrows: yet we did esteem him stricken, smitten of God, and afflicted. But he was wounded for our transgressions, he was bruised for our iniquities: the chastisement of our peace was upon him; and with his stripes we are healed. All we like sheep have gone astray; we have turned every one to his own way; and the Lord hath laid on him the iniquity of us all.
>
> He was oppressed, and he was afflicted, yet he opened not his mouth: he is brought as a lamb to the slaughter, and as a sheep before her shearers is dumb, so he openeth not his mouth. He was taken from prison and from judgment: and who shall declare his generation? for he was cut off out of the land of the living: for the transgression of my people was he stricken. And he made his grave with the wicked, and with the rich in his death; because he had done no violence, neither was any deceit in his mouth. (Isaiah 53:3–9 KJV)

By now you should have guessed it: I am talking about Jesus. When one considers all that Jesus went through, how could it not at least challenge or test His self-esteem as a man? Would it not affect or challenge yours? I know that He was God, but He was also fully human and faced the same temptations that you and I face. Hebrews 4:15 says, "For we do not have a high priest who is unable to sympathize with our weaknesses, but we have one who in every respect has been tested as we are, yet without sin." He was tested, but He did not sin. He did not sin because Jesus did not embrace false identity or image that others were projecting upon Him. To embrace a false you is sin! Jesus was tested just as we are, yet He did not SIN! In other words, He had the victory and so can you and I!

The Scriptures clearly teach that Jesus was tested. Only two things kept His esteem in tact: He knew who He was, and He knew what His divine purpose and mission were. Self-knowledge in God is the key to overcoming LSE. Jesus knew that He was the Son of Man and the Son of God. Jesus knew that He and the Father were one. So because He knew who He was, others' opinions of Him may have hurt, but it did not cause Him to lose His focus. Jesus understood His mission and purpose. He also knew that His suffering was a part of this mission. So He hung there on the cross until He cried, "It is finished!"

"But he was wounded for our transgressions, he was bruised for our iniquities: the chastisement of our peace was upon him; and with his stripes we are healed" (Isaiah 53:5 KJV).

Beloved, Jesus is a healer. He not only heals us of

LSE, but His life clearly demonstrates for us how we can be victorious over LSE by understanding who we are in Him and by fulfilling God's divine purpose and calling for us. Healing comes with a relationship and a closer walk with Jesus.

NOTES

[8] Walter Winks, *Unmasking the Powers* (Philadelphia: Fortress Press, 1986), 46.

CHAPTER V

The Survey

To test the theory of my thesis, I conducted a mini-survey. The following survey was given to the members of the Concord Missionary Baptist Church, the Woodlawn Organization, and the District 89 school system teachers. I also asked them to give the survey to their co-workers. We passed out one hundred surveys, fifteen of which were completed and returned to me within the requested timeframe. It is a small sample, but the results are still insightful and worth sharing.

Sample Survey

Instructions: **Do not put your name on this survey**. Please answer each question as openly and honestly as possible. Feel free to use additional pages for your answers if necessary. Please return no later than Sunday, June 3, 2001. Thank you for your participation and honesty. If you have any questions, please don't hesitate to ask.

1. Gender: a) Male   b) Female

2. Age Range:
   a) Teenager   b) Young Adult   c) Adult   d) Senior

3. Do you like yourself? Yes   No
   Why or why not?

4. Do you love yourself? Yes   No
   Why or why not?

5. How do you see yourself?

6. What do you think about yourself?

7. How do you feel about yourself?

8. What causes you to see, think, and feel the way you do about yourself?

9. What can the Ministry do to improve the way you see, think, or feel about yourself?

Survey Results:

We had a fifteen-percent return rate. Out of one hundred given out, fifteen were returned.

Interpretation of the Results

Over ninety-seven percent of the respondents said they liked and/or loved themselves. This is very surprising and somewhat encouraging to me. If this is true, those with positive self-esteem can help encourage those with low self-esteem. Also encouraging is that most of the professionals, especially the teachers, had a healthy sense of self. They found their esteem in their positions and in their professional achievements. Most of them felt that the community and social institutions, such as the family, supported their self-esteem.

But I wonder what I would have found if I had probed a little deeper. I think many people say they love themselves, but I wonder how they really feel about themselves?

It was also interesting to note that many of them felt that the ministry (another institutional role) could help in developing their self-esteem by teaching, preaching, and encouraging.

Of those who admitted they had esteem issues, they cited the source of their LSE was the perception given to them by parents, family, others, community, and life experiences.

Our findings are consistent with others who have done research in the area of esteem and what contributes to one's self worth and value.

CHAPTER VI

Transformed Esteem— The Rebirth of the Real You

∞

The following is an excerpt from an email that I received from my mother's sister, Aunt Vivian, who reviewed an earlier manuscript of the book. I have elected to include it here because it describes in detail her transformation experience from LSE:

Good Morning Dear,

I just finished listening to your sermon (entitled "Just Be Yourself!"). Man, that was awesome; I had to get a little praise in on that one!

Now, let's get to the book. I really enjoyed what you've written so far. While reading, a lot of issues and situations from my own life came to mind. And the sad thing is, although I thought I had been delivered from this spirit of low self-esteem, sometimes a simple remark or occurrence can make me feel inadequate.

The thing that changed my perception of "self" was that soft, small voice of God telling me simply, "Vivian, I love you!" Kenneth, we were living in Georgia, and I was sitting at the dining room table folding up clothes one night as James and Jamie slept. I wasn't down, I wasn't going through anything ... in fact, compared to some of the emotional highs and lows I'd been through (say in the five to eight years prior to this), I was doing pretty good. As I sat there I heard, "Vivian, I love you." I looked around, you see, I knew that I was the only one awake, so I wanted to see who had spoken to me. I didn't see anyone, so I dismissed it. Then He spoke again, not louder, but with a little more persistence: "Vivian, I love you!" Then, a warmth overtook me, and it felt as if God was literally embracing me with His arms!!! All I could do was weep and praise His name!!!

It's one thing to read the Word and know intellectually that God loves you, because that's what it says and we know His word is real and true. But when He makes it personal ... man, I haven't been the same since!!!"

VR

For Aunt Vivian, her deliverance and transformation came in a *kairos* (Greek for an eternal or godly unit of time) moment, when she really was not expecting it. Her comments also reveal the reality of the continual struggle not to return to the place of torment that LSE can bring.

Wartburg College

My transformation did not occur in a *kairos* moment, but it was a process. For me, it was several moments, beginning in 1985. In August of 1985, I barely graduated from Wartburg in Waverly, Iowa. The only good news was that I did graduate. Earlier that June, I had the privilege of marching with the Class of 1985. I shall never forget that day, because I was one of only three Black (we were Black then, not African American!) students to graduate that year. Of the three, I was the only one of African American descent. The other two were from Africa. When we started four years before, there were twenty-two Black students. Many people thought I would never make it. There were times when even I thought I would not make it. But I thank God that I did.

The two most important lessons I learned from that experience were to always believe in myself and to have faith in God. As long as there is a possibility, never, ever give up. It is really not over until God declares it is over or until you quit. How tragic it is that many people give up prematurely. Unfortunately for some, the very minute that trial and tribulation challenge or contest their dreams, they choose to abort them and abandon their mission. I thought about leaving Wartburg several times. Once during my junior year of college, I called home and started complaining about all of my troubles and struggles with school, basketball, and girls. My mother just listened and finally said,

"Why don't you come on home and take drum lessons? It would be a lot cheaper for me!" Once I thought about the absurdness of her comment and how close I was to completing my degree, I decided I had better stay in school and finish.

I know that it is very difficult to keep hoping when you are overwhelmed with despair. Sometimes it is easier to quit than to keep trying. But if God gives you the vision, He will also give you the provision to bring it to pass. My success in school and in life was a community effort. With the help of God, friends, professors, and family, I made it.

Real Life Work

Like all my other "firsts," we celebrated. But the celebration didn't last too long, because after school comes life.... Reality.... Work.... After sending out resume after resume and getting rejection after rejection, my self-esteem once again took another serious beat-down.

Here I was a college graduate with a degree in computer science, owing thousands of dollars in student loans, and no job! After several months of rejection, my mother's friend Zonobia in Cincinnati suggested that I come live with her and she would help me to find a job. I figured that I had nothing to lose, so I decided to move to Cincinnati, Ohio. I ended up taking a job at the Cincinnati Computer Store. I will never forget my initial interview. The store manager, Ron Eldrich, took a look at my résumé and then me and said, "You are Black. Why should I hire you?" On the inside, I was hurt and angry. If we were in the streets, I would have let him have it. But my spirit would not let me respond with hurt, anger, or malice. So I simply said, "Well, the reason you should hire me is because I can reach people and get in doors that you can't because you are White." He smiled and said, "You have the job. When do you want to start?" I said, "Wait a minute—what's the starting salary?" He said, "It'll be $2.50 per hour plus commission." I thought to myself, "Here I am a college grad and most of my classmates are making $25,000.00 or more, and I am making minimum wage plus commission!" But I didn't have a job, and I needed the money and the experience. Besides, I learned that any job that is honest, legitimate, and uplifts humanity is worth doing. Even though I wasn't making a lot of money, I felt good about myself. I looked forward to putting on a suit, going to work, and putting in an honest day's work. It really felt good. And since I did not have any other options, it was worth it. An honest job is better than no job. And little did I know that in that same job, God would be preparing me for bigger and better things. I didn't have a clue that I would be blessed beyond my wildest imagination. In that minimum-wage job, I was introduced to the love of my life, Veneeta K. Brewster. I never would have met her had I not been in that job. It is so important to be in the right place at the right time to receive your blessings. Shortly after I met her and really got saved, the Lord started opening doors. Veneeta and I got married in November of 1986 and it has been uphill every since.

    The Lord started restoring my self-esteem, but then I started trying to live my life vicariously through Veneeta. I always wanted to go to school and get my Master's degree, but I never thought I was smart enough to do so. Now

Veneeta is a very beautiful and intelligent lady. So "my" plan was to take advantage of that. I began encouraging Veneeta to go back to school and get her Masters in Education. But the more I pushed, the more she resisted. Then one day the Lord told me, "Leave Veneeta alone and quit trying to live your life through her. I have anointed you, and in your season, I shall bless you to develop your mind and go to school."

So I quit pushing her and started working on pursuing my graduate studies. But again, I ran into a brick wall. Every school that I applied to would not accept me because of my undergraduate grades. Although I graduated, my GPA was 2.3 and my GMAT scores were just average. They wanted the cream of the crop. So I just put school on the back burner and continued to work hard at my profession. So I was able to achieve some success at my job. Then I was called to the ministry and my employer relocated us to Chicago. Once again, the desire to go to school came into my spirit. With the support of my late Pastor (Rev. James Fair), my wife, church, and family, I applied for the Masters of Divinity program at NBTS (Northern Baptist Theological Seminary) in Lombard. Much to my surprise, I was accepted. Not only was I accepted, but also a group of the members of the Concord MB Church—led by Pastor James Fair, my mother Mary Marzette, godmother Joyce Jackson, and grandparents Walter and Eleanor Keys—got together and vowed to help me by at least paying for one hour of school per quarter. So not only was I accepted into the MDiv. Program at NBTS, but God had also provided a financial way through His people. It took me eight years to complete the degree, but once again I made it, this time with an above-average GPA of 3.5. Proverbs 13:12 says, "Hope deferred makes the heart sick, but a desire fulfilled is a tree of life." It was rough, but I made it. During this time, we had two lovely children (Morgan and David), I accepted a call to the pastorate, started IMANI Faith Productions, and lost my mother, brother and grandmother, but I made it. During those eight years, God healed me from LSE and developed and restored the confidence that I needed to do the work that He called me to do. By the time this book is published, I will have graduated from NBTS. I owe so much to so many, especially the saints at the world's greatest church, the Concord Missionary Baptist Church, for investing in me. I am also proud to say that Veneeta will have also graduated with her Masters in Educational Administration!

CHAPTER VII

Self-Esteem and Ministry

∞

We wear the mask that grins and lies,
It hides our cheeks and shades our eyes—
This debt we pay to human guile;
With torn and bleeding hearts we smile,
And mouth with myriad subtleties.
Why should the world be overwise,
In counting all our tears and sighs?
Nay, let them only see us, while
We wear the mask.
We smile, but, O great Christ, our cries
To thee from tortured souls arise.
We sing, but oh the clay is vile
Beneath our feet, and long the mile;
But let the world dream otherwise,
We wear the mask!

—*Paul Laurence Dunbar*

One of my associate ministers at the CBC, Minister Marlowe Cribbs, is a very talented songwriter and worship leader. One day while Marlowe and I were sitting and talking in the office, he shared with me this song he wrote which really blessed my soul entitled "My Testimony (Chosen Anyway)." The words are:

> I was never everybody's choice for a football game. All the others guys would laugh at me and say: "Look at him, he's got a small frame."
> Then, somebody would feel sympathy, they would point to me and I would get to play.
> Though I wasn't the people's choice, I was chosen anyway.
> I was never all the ladies' choice for a boyfriend.
> I was the one they would pass by and say: "Excuse me, please. I'm trying to get to him!"
> But then, good men are few and far between, and they notice me but it is too late.
> Although I wasn't the ladies' choice, I was chosen anyway.
>
> (Chorus)
> Counted out and done without
> I was thought to be a second string.
> Overlooked and under foot
> I have been called worse things.
> Folks that said I was no good—When God raised me up,
> They turned around and said: "I knew you would."
> Though I wasn't the people's choice, I was chosen anyway.[9]
>
> —*Marlowe Cribbs*

Self-Esteem and Ministry

I was blessed and shocked by Minister Cribb's testimony, because to see him *boldly* leading praise and worship, one would never think this was his experience. But it is, and it explains with great clarity the anointing he has on his life and his ministry. Romans 5:3–4 says, "We also boast in our sufferings, knowing that suffering produces endurance, and endurance produces character, and character produces hope, and hope does not disappoint us." I also learned that day that Minister Cribbs and I have more in common than I thought. Like Cribbs, I was never the people's choice, but I was chosen anyway! Isn't it awesome that God somehow chooses us, in spite of ourselves?

Everyone has esteem. Everyone has an image and value of oneself. In some professions and vocations, one's esteem is critical to success. Being tri-vocational (an engineer who works with lawyers and sales people, a minister, and an entrepreneur—President/CEO of IMANI Faith Productions, Inc.), I have the pleasure of dealing with people from all walks of life. Some of them have tremendous egos. Confidence and sometimes even arrogance are keys to their success. To be successful and survive in the legal profession, the ministry, or the music/entertainment industry, you have to know yourself and, more importantly, believe in yourself. If you do not have self confidence, you will fail. Nowadays, even gospel artists have tremendous egos. Unfortunately they have to, because it is this confidence that sets them apart and establishes the level of excellence that is necessary to be successful at their craft. It is also this confidence that jumpstarts the creativity process and keeps the creative juices flowing.

While in college, I did several professional recordings, although I barely consider myself an amateur musician. I have played the drums on and off for better than twenty years. Although I love music, I cannot tell you how often I was wounded by other musicians who would laugh at me when I messed up.

When I was younger, the minister of music of our church would even ask me to get off the drums when he perceived a better drummer had come into the church. I cannot tell you how badly that hurt. Even after all these years, I still sometimes feel that pain.

So, as a consequence, I would always try to play to impress others, when in reality I was demonstrating my insecurity and immaturity. This happens all the time. All too often, immature musicians, singers, and even preachers get "spooked" when other accomplished individuals grace the room with their presence. The ego makes one attempt to impress by over-singing, playing, or preaching. If I could offer a bit of wisdom, whatever you do, don't ever work or minister to impress others. You should never allow anyone to cause you to lose your focus. All that really matters is that God is pleased with your performance. Stick to the script, unless the Holy Spirit inspires you to do otherwise.

In terms of ministry, the irony for me is when I read the Bible and looked at the ministry of Jesus, I see more humility than arrogance. I see confidence and sometime boldness, but I never see arrogance or cockiness. I believe that ministers of the gospel are called to be humble. Meek, not weak. Unfortunately, our society views the character disposition of meekness and humility as weakness. Therefore,

Self-Esteem and Ministry

meekness is not considered a desirable character trait and many pastors/preachers have become arrogant and untouchable. Consequently some of our pastors are now superstars and celebrities instead of servants. Couple that with the rising number of mega-multimedia ministry "Tele-Pastors" (television pastors), which many pastors and their members are beginning to accept as the standard for preaching, teaching and ministry, really makes for and interesting time to be in ministry!

Now I do not give this commentary as a criticism of the use of technology in ministry or as a slam to mega ministries or the pastors. Nor do I make this commentary to suggest that clergy should not be respected or appreciated. All that I am saying is that pastors everywhere who are laboring in the vineyard (regardless of size of the ministry or popularity) are to be appreciated and are definitely worthy of their hire.

I strongly argue that making idols or superstars out of our pastors is a big mistake. This creates an atmosphere of competition and comparison. The spirit of comparison and competition is very dangerous and has no place in ministry. All pastors who are doing a work for the Master should be encouraged and supported. I was talking with a pastor who was sharing with me his frustration with the fact that some of his church members were faithfully contributing to televangelist ministries by buying tapes, videos, and books, but would not support his tape ministry. Of his members he said, "Doc, they spend hundreds of dollars to go to attend a conference, but will not spend forty dollars to come to my banquet. Man, they will go out and buy tapes, books, and videos, and won't even spend five dollars to support my tape ministry." He is not alone; this is the sentiment of a lot of local pastors whose members support TV ministries, but won't tithe to their local churches or support those who really take care of their souls. Such things should not be. Now I am not saying that you should not support other ministries. Like I said, I have planted financial seeds in other ministries that bless me all the time. I buy books, tapes, and videos. I even attend conferences. But first I tithe to my church, and then I give to others. I take care of home, then I help others. My father-in-law, Deacon Dan Brewster, taught me that principle. He says, "Supporting the local church is like paying rent for your apartment. If you want to stay there, you've got to pay your rent. Even if you go on vacation, the rent and the bills still need to be paid. That's what you owe. Rent and bills don't stop just because you are on vacation. Take care of home first, then go on vacation." Pops is right. And all I'm saying is that whatever you do, take care of your local church first, and by all means take care of the pastor who cares for your soul because that is how you get blessed. Your pastor may not say it, but all of these things affect the minister and wounds their self-esteem.

Wounded Healers

Pastors are "wounded healers" and yet many of them suffer from LSE. In fact many ministers enter into ministry with LSE. Their infirmities are further compounded and infected by the battle scares of daily life in ministry. That is why it is so important for ministers to allow God to heal their self-esteem before entering ministry. Because once you enter ministry, the focus will be on others at the expense of your self. And one cannot effectively minister to others, when they are seriously wounded themselves!

Furthermore you will be tested. Pastors are not exempt from words of condemnation, past failures, guilt and shame. Pastors are human. They are constantly tested and tempted just like a layperson, in fact even more so. Yet pastors are expected to help heal hurting congregations, when they themselves have been wounded and are in need of healing themselves.

There is a great need for pastoral care for pastors. All pastors need a pastor. Now more that ever, our pastors need prayer. We also need resources and support networks for our infirmities. Pastors need a place that they can go to be ministered to, so that they may come back and be an effective wounded healer. Finally every pastor needs a sabbatical, a period of rest, to allow time for their own wounds to heal. It is in the best interest of every congregation to afford their pastor this privilege and time off from ministry to heal. Because the body is only as strong as the head and if the head is infected, the body will be sick too.

For years, I was trying to find myself as a minister and preacher. My Homiletics Professor at NBTS, Dr. Alfloyd Butler, suggests that to develop the preacher in you, you must not only preach, but also listen to and draw from a variety of preaching traditions and styles. So I would listen to everybody, including best and worst preachers. I would try to emulate my favorite preachers. My church members were not responding to me the way that audiences were responding to the other preachers. I discovered that there is

no anointing or power in emulation or imitation. Then God revealed to me that He did not want me to emulate or impersonate anyone except His Son, Jesus. God wanted me to be me. You see, God knew all about me before He called, anointed, and appointed me. He knew about my shortcomings, failures, and fears. God just wanted me to be Kenneth D. Phelps! So for years, I wasted time and energy trying to be someone else when all God wanted was for me to be myself. And believe it or not, that is what most people want—authenticity in their ministers! They want the real person, not an imitation, duplication, or replica. They want the real thing. And God wants authenticity. Just be yourself, and that is when the anointing will come. That is when the preaching and teaching power will come and lives will be changed!

Beloved, do not ever compare yourself to others. Stop comparing your ministry to other ministries. The spirit of comparison is very dangerous and has no place in ministry. If you aren't careful, you will think that you are a failure in ministry if you don't have at least one thousand members, when an average church has between fifty to one hundred members! If you are not careful, you will think that you are a failure if you do not have a multimedia ministry. If you aren't careful, you will think that you are a failure in preaching if people aren't slain in the spirit, shouting, or coming and laying money at your feet! Your ministry should not be measured by how people respond to you. The measure of your ministry should be how faithful you are to the flock to whom God has entrusted you. Your ministry will be measured by how faithful and committed you and your members are to God.

My good friend and brother Dr. Michael Noble, the pastor of the historic Olivet Baptist Church of Chicago, Illinois, suggests that pastors should not measure the success of their ministries by numbers. He says, "Churches are the flock of God. Shepherds do not measure their flocks by their number, but by their weight. The flocks are measured by how much wool they produce, not by how many sheep they have!" In other words, a church flock should not be measured by the size of the congregation, edifice, or annual income. Churches should be measured by their faithfulness to the Lord and His work! Every church, regardless of size, should ask these questions: Are we producing? Are we producing church members or world changers? Are we producing victims or victors? What are we producing consumers or producers? Are we producing disciples?

One More Thing!

Never let your ego make decisions for you in ministry or in life. The ego can be a dangerous thing if not kept under control.

I live in Chicago, and the winters in the Windy City can be brutally cold. Oftentimes I would take the commuter train downtown to work. One day a few years ago, I left home in a hurry on the coldest day of the year without a scarf and hat. It must have been about twenty below zero, with a deathly cold windchill, and I didn't have anything to protect my head or my neck. As soon as I got downtown, the first thing I did was stop at the first men's clothing store to purchase a hat and a scarf.

Made in His Image

As soon as I got inside the store, I was met by a salesperson who greeted me and then asked if he could help. I told him I was looking for a hat and a scarf. He proceeded to show me where they were located. He then asked me if I was looking for wool or cashmere. I said cashmere. The salesperson then started to tell me that he had just come back from a cashmere conference in Alaska. He took a moment to show me the differences in the scarves and let me feel them. Honestly, I did not care—I just wanted a cheap scarf to keep my neck warm until I got home. I took one of the scarves and then I looked for a price tag, but there was none. I should have known I was in trouble, but I did not have a clue. So I asked the salesperson the price of the scarf. And he said, "Two hundred twenty-five dollars." I must have looked shocked, because he asked, "Is there a problem?" I quickly said, "No, no problem." He asked, "Then which one would you like?" I said, "Do you have one in black?" He replied, "No." I thought to myself, wow, I'm off the hook! I then said, "Well, I am looking for a solid one in black," and I thanked him for his time. I left the store and went to Filene's Basement and purchased a twenty-dollar scarf. Now let me be clear: If he had had it in black, I would have purchased it. I did not have the money on me or in the bank, but I would have charged it. Even though I couldn't afford it, I would have purchased it for my ego's sake. My ego would have made me do it. You see, a symptom of my LSE was that I never wanted anyone, not even strangers, to think I could not afford things. I don't know why, but it was important to me that others know that I was just as good as anyone else. So I would have done it for my ego's sake.

Never let your ego make decisions for you.

Unfortunately, this happens every day. Many people make foolish decisions at the expense of others and their own self esteem. If you are in leadership, never respond or make decisions when somebody bruises your ego because it will ultimately lead to an abuse of power and cause more harm than good. Before you make decisions, always ask yourself why. Check your motives. If it is to make yourself feel better (at the expense of others) or to impress others, that is the wrong motivation. Don't do it. Never let your ego or your flesh make decisions for you.

NOTES

[9] Marlowe Cribbs, "Chosen Anyway."

CHAPTER VIII

Stages of Transformation

∞

Take Off the Mask

Take off the mask.
Don't be afraid.
Take of the mask.
See who you really are.
Take off the mask.
And discover that God is in you!
Take off the mask.
Let others see the beauty that really lies beyond
the mask.

Kenneth D. Phelps © 2002 IMANI Publishing

As I have already mentioned before, sometimes the transformation from low to middle or high self-esteem can be prompted by an event or occasion, while at other times it is a process. In either case, the stages of transformation are the same. There are four stages to transformation of one's self-esteem: (1) awakening, (2) enlightening, (3) embracing, and (4) enrichment.

**Graphic #6
Stages of Transformation**

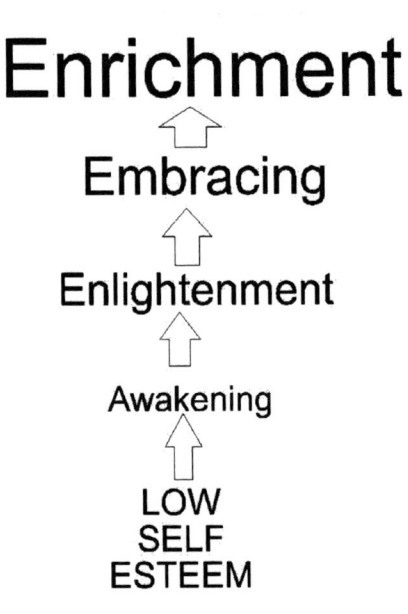

Enrichment
⇧
Embracing
⇧
Enlightenment
⇧
Awakening
⇧
LOW
SELF
ESTEEM

Stage 1. Awakening

The awakening occurs when God gets your attention. It is a rebirth. This usually happens when you are at a point when you have no choice but to see and hear from God. The awakening is the point of revelation when God speaks to you. For Moses, it was the burning bush. For Isaiah, it was the death of Uzziah. For Paul, it was the Damascus Road experience, and for Elijah, it was the still quiet voice within. For me, I woke up one morning and realized that things that used to matter didn't matter any longer. I woke up and realized that I was made in the likeness and image of God.

Stage 2. Enlightening

The enlightening is the second stage of the transformation. This is when the revelation is articulated and you understand the voice of God. It is when you discover the truth of who you are in Him. During this stage, you also understand a little more about your mission and purpose. Each of us has a divine God-given mission and purpose in life. And we do not leave here until our life work is complete.

It is also at this stage when you understand who you are. Listen, beloved, when you really understand who you are in Christ, you will no longer devalue yourself or allow others to devalue you. When you really understand who you are in Christ, you no longer abuse or torment yourself by replaying painful memories in your mind. Nor will you accept abuse or torment from others! When you really understand who you are in Christ, those people, places, and things that used to intimidate you will be intimidated by you. When you really understand who you are, you will no longer allow yourself to be hooked up with people who are detrimental to you and your spiritual health. When you really understand who you are in Christ and, more importantly, your value to the kingdom, the enemy, the devil himself, becomes terrified!

Stage 3. Embracing

Next is the embracing. In this stage of the transformation process, you accept the truth and become compelled and driven to live by it. Many people know the truth but aren't living by it.

I think that a practical example would best serve us here. While on a return flight from Dallas, I met a preacher by the name of Stephanie. It was an early flight, so I slept most of the way. But when I woke up, I decided to edit my manuscript. As I flipped through the pages, I could tell that she was trying to read the manuscript, but I didn't say anything. Finally she got up enough courage to ask me what I was working on. So I told her that I working on a book about low self-esteem.

She asked, "What's the title?"
I replied, *"Made in His Image."*
She asked, "Oh, are you a Christian?"
I responded, "Yes."
She then asked, "Are you a minister?"
I said, "Yes."
She exclaimed, "Wow, me too."

What transpired from this point on was incredible and worth sharing. It was as if I had a divine appointment, and her story was to be included in this book. Stephanie shared with me as if I had known her for years. She told me that her mother died when she was twelve years old, and that she was raised by her sisters. Her sisters taught her that sex was wrong and if she got pregnant, she could not live at home any more, and she believed them. Shortly thereafter, in high school, she met the love of her life, but she could not see him because her sisters would not allow it. So she graduated from high school and went to college. Her high-school sweetheart followed her to the same college. Initially it was great because they could openly pursue their love for one another without sibling interference. Finally the unthinkable happened—Stephanie got pregnant. She was so ashamed and depressed. In fact, she said it took her eight months to share with her sisters that she was pregnant. She finally went home to have the baby. They didn't put her out, but they made it very difficult for her and made her feel guilty.

After having the baby, she decided to drop out of college. This decision sent Stephanie into an extreme depression. She did eventually marry the baby's daddy, her high-school sweetheart, but they had problems because she did not want to get pregnant again, and it affected their relationship. Consequently, he began to cheat on her and their marriage ended. She said to me, "I feel like a failure. I never complete anything. The only good things in my life are my relationships with God and my daughter. I am not happy with what I'm doing. I don't like the way I look. I feel I'm too fat." She then confessed to me that she had never told anyone what she had just shared with me.

Here was a saved woman, a preacher, who was carrying all that baggage, that guilt, shame, and sense of failure. She did it for more than twenty years. She had been a minister for some time, encouraging other women, but she never knew that what she was giving to others was also available to her. In other words, she failed to embrace the truth that Jesus forgives, saves, heals, delivers, and sets free. She preached forgiveness and healing, but she could not bring herself to accept the same grace that she was sharing with others.

The Spirit told me to simply say to her, "Daughter, thy sins have been forgiven. Rise, take up your bed, and walk! This is the first step to your breakthrough. God is going to turn your misery into your ministry, and many shall be healed by your testimony." With tears streaming down her face, I believe that she embraced her healing.

The plane landed at Midway Airport in Chicago and we disembarked. I was in a hurry to get to our Youth Ministry's Senior Mission outing, so I hastened to get my luggage. I then thought it would be nice to say good-bye to Stephanie, so I looked for her at the baggage carousel, but she was nowhere to be found. She seemed to have disappeared. It was as if she was an angel.

I don't know where Stephanie is, but I know that in the moments that we shared, God removed a heavy burden from her.

Stephanie's situation is hurtful, and I know this because I was in the same situation during college. My mother gave me the same lecture as Stephanie's sisters did. However, after three years of college, it happened. I got a friend pregnant, while home visiting one weekend. I felt guilty and thought that I had messed up my life. But the good news is that God forgave me, and so did my mother. I'm sure that she was disappointed and possibly hurt, but she never, ever stopped loving and supporting me. In fact, that whole ordeal made us closer instead of tearing us apart. For years I carried that guilt and felt that any time something bad happened to me, I deserved it, because of what I did years ago. I now know that it wasn't a mistake. I now know that the act that leads to conception was a sin and a lack of discipline on my part, but the child was not a mistake. Children are not mistakes! Children are precious gifts from God. God forgave me years ago, but it was not until a few years ago that I allowed myself to be forgiven.

He could do the same thing for you. Listen, your salvation includes the forgiveness of sin. Past hurts, failures, and shortcomings no longer have dominion over you. Embrace that fact and be healed!

Stage 4. Enrichment

The final stage of transformation is enrichment. This is when you build up your esteem. It occurs as you walk with the Lord in the vocation to which you are called. Enrichment happens as you pray, study, worship, and disciple others. It is not enough to just know who you are, but you have an obligation to build on that revelation and go disciple others. I think that is what Jesus meant when He said to Peter, "When thou art converted, strengthen thy brethren" (Luke 22:32 KJV). Exercise, success, and achievement build confidence.

CHAPTER IX

Forgiveness:
The Doorway to Healing

∞

Therefore is the kingdom of heaven likened unto a certain king, which would take account of his servants. And when he had begun to reckon, one was brought unto him, which owed him ten thousand talents. But forasmuch as he had not to pay, his lord commanded him to be sold, and his wife, and children, and all that he had, and payment to be made. The servant therefore fell down, and worshipped him, saying, Lord, have patience with me, and I will pay thee all. Then the lord of that servant was moved with compassion, and loosed him, and forgave him the debt.

But the same servant went out, and found one of his fellowservants, which owed him an hundred pence: and he laid hands on him, and took him by the throat, saying, Pay me that thou owest. And his fellowservant fell down at his feet, and besought him, saying, Have patience with me, and I will pay thee all. And he would not: but went and cast him into prison, till he should pay the debt. So when his fellowservants saw what was done, they were very sorry, and came and told unto their lord all that was done.

Then his lord, after that he had called him, said unto him, O thou wicked servant, I forgave thee all that debt, because thou desiredst me: Shouldest not thou also have had compassion on thy fellowservant, even as I had pity on thee? And his lord was wroth, and delivered him to the tormentors, till he should pay all that was due unto him.

So likewise shall my heavenly Father do also unto you, if ye from your hearts forgive not every one his brother their trespasses. (Matthew 18:23–35 KJV)

And forgive us our debts, as we forgive our debtors.... For if ye forgive men their trespasses, your heavenly Father will also forgive you: But if ye forgive not men their trespasses, neither will your Father forgive your trespasses. (Matthew 6:12, 14, 15 KJV)

In the eighteenth chapter of the gospel of Matthew, Jesus told His disciples the parable of a servant who begged for mercy and was forgiven a great debt by his master. The servant, in turn, refused to release or forgive someone who owed him a much lesser debt. In fact, the parable suggests that he physically seized him by his throat and took him to court to be judged, insisting on a much harsher judgment and punishment than would be required for a lesser debt or crime. The servant's action and his refusal to forgive were reported to the servant's master. The master then summoned him and questioned him concerning his harsh behavior. Not receiving a reasonable response, the master reinstated the servant's original penalty for his debt and sentenced him to a life of torment for his unwillingness to have mercy and forgive.

Wow! The message of the parable is clear: those who have been forgiven should also forgive. In other words, it is a sin not to forgive, and those who refuse to forgive will be held accountable!

I have been in the ministry for over twelve years. I have found that for some strange reason, it always seems so difficult for the forgiven to forgive. In my experience with most church folks, forgiveness is not practiced. It is not even in their vocabulary. The forgiveness of trespasses or debts unfortunately is a rare occasion in the household of faith. I have found that forgiveness is not the norm. In fact, it is almost as if it is considered a sin to forgive. In the majority of my counseling sessions or Bible study groups, whenever the topic of forgiveness surfaces, it is often met with resistance and sometime rage.

This is most unfortunate, because unforgiveness is like a cancer; if left untreated, it will cause further sickness to the body and ultimately death. Unforgiveness renders the body impotent and very weak. Unforgiveness affects our relationship with God and man. The pews in our churches are filled with congregants who hold grudges and simply refuse to forgive each other. This is one of the reasons why the church is not as powerful as she should be.

On several occasions I have asked, "Why is it so difficult to forgive?" I have never gotten a reasonable response to this question. So I have concluded that there are a few possible reasons why people don't forgive. First of all, they do not forgive because they have not been taught to do so. Most people have not been taught the power of forgiveness. Another reason why people don't forgive is because they understand forgiveness involves relinquishing hatred. In most cases, unforgiveness results in a separation or loss of a relationship with someone who is near and dear to them. And to forgive, in their minds, means or translates into the loss of the final piece of that relationship or control. They embrace the myth that to forgive either means that they have to restore the relationship to its original state (which can really be painful) or move on. In either case, it is very difficult to do. So hatred and unforgiveness are easier than peace and love. But the truth of the matter is that relinquishing or forgiving the debt really brings greater freedom and victory.

Another possible reason is a misunderstanding of forgiveness. Most people use the terms "forgive" and "forget" interchangeably. I was taught that to forgive means to forget, which is wrong. "Forgiveness" is defined as a release from debt. "Forget" is defined as erasing from memory. The only one who is able to forgive and forget is God. We forgive and we remember. We never forget, especially when pain and hurt are involved. Although we never forget, we are

Forgiveness: The Doorway to Healing

able to forgive and move on, and that is the real goal of forgiveness. We also think that to forgive means to restore a relationship, but that is also simply not true—it can be, but it doesn't always have to be so. Some people have hurt me and I have hurt others. We have forgiven each other, but the relationships have never been the same again. And that's okay. I have learned that you are free to forgive the other person but never again reach the status of intimacy and closeness you once enjoyed. And that's alright. You have more options than love or hate, you can choose to forgive.

A practical example would best serve us here. In a recent conversation with my Aunt Vivian, she shared with me an embarrassing and painful childhood experience that happened over forty years ago. I asked for permission to write about her experience, and she granted it.

Aunt Vivian and Aunt Roslyn (RoRo) often go to the local mall to walk for exercise. On a recent visit to the mall, they ran into one of their elementary school teachers. In describing the occasion, Aunt Vivian said to me, "Kenneth, when I recognized the teacher, I was overcome with rage and anger." I asked her why. Suddenly Aunt Vivian began to cry, and she confessed, "When I was in the fifth grade, one day at recess, I was playing with my friend who happened to be a boy. I said to one of my girlfriends that he was my boyfriend, not meaning anything romantic, but just that he was a friend who happened to be a boy. My teacher reprimanded me in front of all my classmates. She slapped me and told me to never say that again. Kenneth, I felt so embarrassed and afraid. In fact, I have never shared this with anyone until today. When I saw her, all my anger and hurt resurfaced and

I couldn't stand to be in the presence of that lady. RoRo went to talk to her, but I could not bring myself to face her. In fact, I am not ever going back there again, because if I see her, I don't know what I would do." The Lord told me to say to her, "Aunt Vivian, I'm so sorry that happened to you. It wasn't your fault, and you didn't deserve that." Then the Spirit told me to tell her to go back to the mall when she is ready. Go back to the place of hurt and the place of pain, and there she will find healing and release.

You see, for Aunt Vivian, the original incident and this situation were defining moments in the development of her esteem as a child and as an adult. That experience was so painful that she never forgot it—she repressed it, but she never forgot it. Furthermore, she had never forgiven this teacher for slapping her, and that unfortunate situation was held hostage in her spirit all these years.

I then asked her if she was okay. She said yes, and thanked me. Then we ended the conversation and hung up the phone.

Two weeks later, I called to check on Aunt Vivian and she said, "Kenneth, guess what? I went back." I asked, "Back where?" She responded, "I did what you suggested. I finally got up enough courage to go back to the mall." I asked, "Really! How did it go?" She said, "At first it was really hard—it was if I had a ton of bricks on my shoulders. But the more I walked, the more liberated I became, until finally I felt the burden totally gone. I was healed, delivered, and set free. I feel so good. I thank God for my healing and you for sharing your manuscript with me, because God used your manuscript to heal me."

Forgiveness: The Doorway to Healing

I believe that Aunt Vivian's experience had an impact on her esteem. Unfortunately, we all have painful memories of issues and situations that wounded our self-esteem. Many experiences and images are imprinted into the very corridors of our minds and spirits. Unfortunately, these experiences and images are negative and they wound the very essence of who we are. These negative experiences and images are often produced by words of condemnation, abuse, and neglect from those individuals we love and trust or by those who are in authority over us. Words of condemnation, destructive criticism, and harsh judgment wound our esteem and produce LSE. That is why we need to always think before we speak or act. Contrary to popular belief, words do hurt. If we are ever going to be healed, we must be willing to forgive and be forgiven.

Unforgiveness is a sin and always impedes the healing process and your anointing! In Matthew 6:12, Jesus encourages us to forgive those who have hurt us. He commands us to forgive our debtors. Who are our debtors? Does that mean that we forgive those who owe us money? I believe that the word "debt" can be translated into the word "sin." So we can interpret the text to mean, "Forgive us for our sins, as we forgive those who sin against us." When individuals wound us either intentionally or unintentionally, they sin against us, and whether they ask for forgiveness or not, we are to forgive them. This is not an option—it is a commandment.

We also forgive even though they do not deserve it. Honestly, none of us deserve to be forgiven! But we forgive because it is in our best interest to forgive those who hurt us.

We must name the sin and the sinner and be willing to confront and forgive both. Make a list and begin the journey to forgiveness today.

Beloved, we forgive not because they deserve it. But we forgive because we deserve it. We deserve to be free of debt and debtors! Forgiveness by definition means to release the debt. It is not easy, but when we forgive, it heals us and enables us to live victorious lives. The more you practice forgiveness, the better you will become at it. It is in our best interest to forgive, and not to forgive is a sin that keeps us in bondage. While you are forgiving others, by all means, if necessary, whatever you do, do not forget to forgive yourself. For some of us, the guilt of past failures and mistakes can be overwhelming. The initial step toward self-healing is self-forgiveness. For both self and others, forgiveness is the doorway to healing.

THE FINAL CHAPTER X

It's Not Over—
It's Just Beginning!

∞

New Beginning

Sometimes in life it's hard to start all over.
You thought you had it all but you had nothing.
So you made up in your mind that the sun would never shine,
But then the Lord stepped right in on time.
I used to be messed up on the road heading going the wrong way,
One day Jesus stepped in and dark nights turned into brighter days,
Had to change the way I was walking,
Change the way I was talking,
A new beginning, starting all over again![10]

—*Hugh "Teddy" Jackson, Leon "Rock" Guyton, and Montage Pheloan*

Self-esteem strongly influences the individual and the community. Furthermore, LSE can have devastating effects on the individual, the community, and one's ministry. The results of low self-esteem are abuse and defeat.

Jesus said, "And you will know the truth, and the truth will make [set] you free" (John 8:32). God has already provided a practical answer to low self-esteem, and I believe that it is found in the great commandments: Love God with all your heart, soul, and mind, and your neighbor as yourself. Listen, it is so hard to love God or anyone else when you do not love or respect yourself. This is the first step toward a healthy self-esteem.

The next thing that must happen is a transformation of the individuals' minds by embracing the truth that they are created in God's image and likeness and that they are fearfully and wonderfully made. In other words, "God doesn't make junk!" Beloved, we are made in the express image and likeness of God! That means that humans reflect God's self. We are not God, but we are to be a reflection of Him. We are to look like and act like God in the flesh, Jesus the Christ. Like God, each human can think, choose, feel, respond, initiate, create, and act. Like God, we have the power to speak things into existence as long as they line up with God's will. Sin distorts the image, but faith and holiness correct it. And when God made you, He took great care and consideration. You are a designer original. Never forget that. When you look in the mirror of your life, you should see Christ's reflection. Beloved, you are a precious gift from God. Allow yourself to embrace that image.

Recently while ministering at a church, a beautiful

middle-aged lady came up to me after the service and acknowledged that she could relate to my testimony. Then she confessed that she had been wounded by words of condemnation and suffered from LSE. She said, "All my life, I've been called fat, black, and ugly. Although my husband says he loves me and that I am beautiful, I still see myself as fat, black, and ugly." With tears welling up in her eyes, she said, "I can see clearly now that I am Black, but I am not fat and ugly—I am fearfully and wonderfully made in His image and likeness!" Bless His name! And so are you. You are a gift from the Lord.

At an individual level, each person must affirm this fact. Parents and leaders must see children as gifts from God and that they are precious in His sight. Having this understanding will influence the policies and programs that help to nurture and develop our youth. Furthermore, it is the responsibility of parents and society to affirm positive behavior and to be consistently caring to correct destructive behavior. It is often said, "You can't bend an old tree straight or teach an old dog new tricks," but when it comes to deliverance from LSE, adults can be re-educated and change their mirrors (their self-images) by embracing God's reflection. This requires faith! Receiving this transformation requires believing in spite of what family, community, and others have projected upon you. It requires relinquishing the guilt of past shame, hurts, failures, mistakes, and shortcomings.

At a communal or societal level, all institutions (schools, churches, businesses, and governmental agencies) must take full responsibility for the part they play in the mass destruction of our self-esteem. Therefore, we must repent and vow as institutions and communities to change our perceptions of the community. Each institution must be responsible for discovering and uncovering the truth about the community it serves. As communities, we must also vow not to embrace negative reflections of us as portrayed in the media, even if it means pooling our collective resources and creating our own images based upon positive perceptions and healthy values.

One example of that is found in lyrical content of the acoustic lyricist India Aries. Listen to the words to her popular R&B song "Video":

Video

Verse 1
Sometimes I shave my legs and sometimes I don't
Sometimes I comb my hair and sometimes I won't
Depend of how the wind blows I might even paint my toes
It really just depends on whatever feels good in my soul

Verse 2
When I look in the mirror and the only one there is me
Every freckle on my face is where it's suppose to be
And I know my creator didn't make no mistakes on me
My feet, my thighs, my Lips, my eyes, I'm loving what I see

Chorus
I'm not the average girl from your video
And I ain't built like a supermodel
But I learned to love myself unconditionally,
Because I am a queen

I'm not the average girl from your video
My worth is not determined by the price of my clothes
No matter what I'm wearing I will always be India.Arie[11]

We need more songs like "Video," "Chosen Anyway," and "New Beginning," which promote self-love and not self-destruction. The music and the arts are powerful mechanisms to project any image or vision that one deems as valid. Gangster rappers justify their lyrics under the banner of free speech and by claiming that they promote reality. They claim that the key to their commercial success is the power of the masses to relate to their vision of reality. But I challenge our artists to change the vision. And I admonish them not to gain the whole world at the expense of the souls of the masses. I would challenge them to be more prophetic and artistically responsible by promoting a healthy vision for our community. "For where there is no vision, the people perish." What we need is a vision for America that builds the community instead of tearing it down. We need one rooted in the fact that we are all reflections of the image of God and are made in His likeness.

It is not over; it's just the beginning!

Through out the book I have shared a lot of ideas, thoughts and information regarding LSE and how to overcome low self-esteem. Whenever I teach or preach on any subject, most people find it very helpful, when I summarize the important points of the lesson or sermon at the end.

Let me close this work, by saying that,

- LSE can and will victimize any individual or community willing to embrace and nurture it. LSE is no respecter of person.
- LSE is a sin. It is a sin, because it is sinful to hate what God Loves. And beloved God does love you and he desires for you to love you too!

If you are a victim of LSE, the following steps will facilitate your healing.

Step 1: If you do not have personal relationship with Jesus, establish one today! This is done by confessing your sins to God and believing that Jesus Christ is the Savior of the world. Romans 10:9 says, " That if thou shalt confess with thy mouth the Lord Jesus, and shalt believe in thine heart that God hath raised him from the dead, thou shalt be saved.".

Step 2: Allow your self to forgive and be forgiven. Make a list of all the people, places and things that have wounded your spirit and contributed to your low self-esteem and forgive them. Be specific and thorough and do not forget to forgive yourself.

Step 3: Change the way you look at your self. See

yourself as God sees you. Define yourself in light of the Word of God. "For *the LORD seeth* not as man seeth; for man looketh on the outward appearance, but the LORD looketh on the heart." 1 Sam 16:7. If you choose to change your outward appearance, that is okay. But let it be your choice and done on your own terms, so that it is pleasing to the Lord and to you too!

Step 4: Defeat the lie with the truth. Do not listen to, embrace or entertain negativity in any form, from others or self. Do not embrace words of condemnation, negative images or concepts that contradicts what God has declared about you. Beloved be careful what you feed your mind and spirit. Surround yourself with positive affirmations and people that build up your spirit and self-esteem. No matter what others say about you, the truth of the matter is that you are fearfully and wonderfully made in his image and likeness!

NOTES

[10] Montage Pheloan and Youth Fellowship, on the CD entitled, "New Beginning," IMANI Faith Productions, Inc., 1998.

[11] India Arie, song entitled "Video" from the CD, *Acoustic Soul* (www.indi-aarie.com).

Bibliography

Aldridge, Jerry, Jr. *Self-Esteem: Loving Yourself at Every Age*. Birmingham: Doxa Books, 1993.

Mitchell, Henry H. and Thomas, Emil M. *Preaching for Black Self-Esteem*. Nashville: Abingdon Press, 1994.

Winks, Walter. *Unmasking the Powers*. Philadelphia: Fortress Press, 1986.

Web Sites:
India Aries:
http://www.indiaarie.com/

Self Image:
http://fox.klte.hu/~keresofi/psychotherapy/a-to-z-entries/selfimage_.html

IMANI Faith Productions: Montage Pheloan and Youth Fellowship:
http://www.imanifaithproductions.com/

About the Author

∞

Rev. Kenneth D. Phelps—
Pastor, Teacher, Author,
Playwright and Entrepreneur

Throughout our lives we are often compared to many things. Our sincere desire is that these representations are vividly illustrated with positive images that flatter our actions, desires, and achievements. Godly men and women are likened in the Scriptures to sturdy trees. From the pulpit, Reverend Kenneth D. Phelps, like the tree, stands straight for God to teach, guide, and protect. A director of deliverance, this is a man who firmly believes in nurturing his flock by providing opportunities and options, like blessings, to those willing to receive them. Among the congregation, he is mentor, friend, partner, and pastor. In times of delight or despair, he shines as a light of hope exemplifying the glory of God's infinite wisdom, strong in his convictions, confident in Christ. "He shall be like a tree planted by the rivers of water, that bringeth forth his fruit in his season" (Psalm 1:3 KJV).

Made in His Image

Concord Missionary Baptist Church (CMBC) is the fertile valley in which Reverend Kenneth D. Phelps thrives and grows in grace. He confessed Christ at an early age. He was licensed to preach in November 1990 and ordained in May 1994. His life-long relationship and devotion to the Lord culminated into a dream fulfilled as he was called to pastor at CMBC on December 19, 1994.

Married for fifteen years to Veneeta B. Phelps, Reverend Kenneth D. Phelps is the father of three beautiful children, Kenneth, Morgan, and David (who are his pride and joy). He holds a B.A. in Computer Information Systems from Wartburg College in Waverly, Iowa, and a Master of Divinity degree from Northern Baptist Theological Seminary. He stands as firm as a tree, committed and guided by the doctrine of faith, giving shade as words to comfort, providing natural resources to build people up in the Lord. He is a blessing to all who know him, bearing the fruits of his labors to feed multitudes.

About IMANI Faith Productions

∞

IMANI symbolizes many things, and is faith by translation, perfection in its application. In the Kwanzaa celebration, IMANI is the seventh and final day, representing God's perfect number and its foundation, symbolizing purity, strength, and stability. This is IMANI Faith Productions.

Founded by Reverend Kenneth D. Phelps and Veneeta D. Phelps, IMANI Faith Productions is a Christian-based recording, publishing, production, and music-entertainment company. As an extension of the ministry of Concord Missionary Baptist Church, IMANI provides opportunities to talented individuals by showcasing, marketing, and developing talent holistically. The IMANI Staff is primarily comprised of church members who lend their gifts to ensure that IMANI is victorious in its mission.

For further information on IMANI Faith Productions or to purchase IMANI Products, visit our Website at: www.imanifaithproductions.com, call us at 630-415-1900, or write us at the following address:

IMANI Faith Productions
P.O. Box 239
Bloomingdale, IL 60108

IMANI Order Form

Date: _____

To: _____
Ship To: _____
Name: _____
Address: _____
_____

City: _____ **St:** _____ **Zip:** _____
Contact: _____
Phone: _____ **Fax:** _____

Qty.	Description/Product Number	Unit price	Amount
	Made in His Image Book (soft cover)	$10.00	
	NuWave So Grateful To You CD	$12.00	
	NuWave So Grateful To You Cassette	$ 8.00	
	Montage Pheloan and YF New Beginning CD	$12.00	
	Montage Pheloan and YF New Beginning Cassette	$ 8.00	
SUBTOTAL			
SALES TAX			
SHIPPING & HANDLING			
TOTAL DUE			

You may send this order form to:
 IMANI Faith Productions, Inc.
 PO Box 239
 Bloomingdale, IL 60108
Or fax it to: 630-293-9813 – Attn.: Sales Dept.

Make all checks payable to: IMANI Faith Productions

If you have any questions concerning this invoice, call Rev. Kenneth D. Phelps, 630-415-1900, ext. 3.

THANK YOU FOR YOUR BUSINESS!

"May God richly bless and keep you" is our prayer.
"Without IMANI, it's impossible to please God!"

Appendix A

Survey

Instructions: ***Do not put your name on this survey***. Please answer each question as openly and honestly as possible. Feel free to use additional pages for your answers if necessary. Please return no later than Sunday, June 3, 2001. Thank you for your participation and honesty. If you have any questions, please don't hesitate to ask.

—Pastor Phelps

1. Gender:
    a) Male
    b) Female

2. Age Range:
    a) Teenager
    b) Young Adult
    c) Adult
    d) Senior

3. Do you like yourself?
   Yes
   No

   Why or Why Not?

4. Do you love yourself?
   Yes
   No

   Why or Why Not?

5. How do you see yourself?

6. What do you think about yourself?

7. How do you feel about yourself?

8. What causes you to see, think, and feel the way you do about yourself?

9. What can the Ministry do to improve the way you see, think, or feel about yourself?

Appendix A

Survey Results

We had a fifteen-percent return rate. Out of one hundred given out, fifteen were returned.

1. Gender:
   a) Male – 3
   b) Female – 12

2. Age Range:
   a) Teenager – 2
   b) Young Adult – 4
   c) Adult – 7
   d) Senior – 2

3. Do you like yourself?
   Yes – 14
   No – 0
   Sometimes – 1

   Why or Why Not?
   "Positive attitude, goals established, and can deal with reality."
   "Sometimes I'm good and sometimes I'm bad."
   "I should like myself. I have to accept the way God made me."
   "Because I am one of God's creatures."
   "I am a good person who tries hard."
   "I am unique."
   "Because God put me on earth for a purpose."
   "I like myself because I'm in excellent heath and I con-

tribute to my community in every way I can."

"Because I know I am somebody and I like the way that God made me."

"Because after messing up my teenage and young adult years, the Lord spoke to me and told me I am better than I was treating myself and my body and that He loved me. I heard Him and listened."

4. Do you love yourself?
   Yes – 14
   No – 0
   Sometimes – 1

   Why or Why Not?
   "I listen to His words and hear them in my heart."
   "I am lovable."
   "I am content with myself, but I have self-love issues."
   "Makes me capable of spreading or extending love to others."
   "Because I'm human and I make mistakes and I've learned to accept all things about me."
   "I love myself and I also love other people."
   "Because God made me fearfully and wonderfully."
   "I'm thankful for where I've been, where I am, and where I'm going."
   "I love myself, because I was loved when I came into the world."
   "I love myself because Christ first loved me and taught me how to love myself."

5. How do you see yourself?
    "I see myself as a pleasant person and a valuable one."
    "Since I am a senior, I try to take care of myself and treat everybody right."
    "Mostly inadequate and fat. I was trained to not like what I saw in the mirror."
    "Mother, teacher, successful and intelligent."
    "As a positive and caring individual."
    "As a progressive individual ('Work in Progress')."
    "A loving and caring person."
    "A leader, mother, friend, professional Christian, optimist."
    "Kind, gifted, attractive."
    "Powerful."
    "A seasoned professional loving son, father, uncle, nephew, and friend."
    "A Christian woman trying to do the work of the Lord. It's hard and a struggle, but I know if I keep my hands in God's hand, I can make it."
6. What do you think about yourself?
    "For the most part, I am a good person with decent morals and high goals."
    "I think I am sweet, sincere, honest, giving, loving, and intelligent."
    "A well-adjusted person who has that sixth sense and can read other people quite well."
    "Hard worker and student."
    "I think about myself as a person."
    "I think about myself as a mother, grandmother, great-great grandmother, and a happy person."

"I think I'm continually growing in wisdom and changing—a work in progress."
"Smart and efficient."
"A good servant."
"I see myself as self-motivated, sincere, and a person of integrity."
"I think I'm a loving, giving, and a kind person, a hard worker, a friendly person."

7. How do you feel about yourself?
    "I am the bomb!"
    "I feel I need to lose weight and hook up with God to feel better. When you know better, you do better."
    "Good."
    "Believe that I am lovable, capable of doing many things and caring."
    "Sometimes good, and sometimes bad."
    "I feel good about myself."
    "I feel that at my age I am not perfect. I make mistakes. I pray for forgiveness also."
    "Blessed (proud) of my growth, my accomplishments (my child, career)."
    "I feel that I am too sensitive."
    "Great."
    "Good, now that I know what God has for me to do on this earth."

8. What causes you to see, think and feel the way you do about yourself?
    "The influences around me, the people in my life."

Appendix A

"Society, family, and how I was raised."
"Surroundings."
"My exposure to many facets of life and various groups of people."
"Wisdom, temptation, and beliefs."
"I thank God for making me."
"I think positive."
"My spiritual self and the reflection of those around me."
"My background and environment. Raised by grandparents and surrounded by good people."
"Because of the way my parents and grandparents reared me."
"Positive thoughts and actions."
"By coming to Sunday school, Bible class, and church, reading the Bible for myself, and praying."
"The changes in my life the feeling that I feel for my fellow man. I love people after being saved. I still sometimes doubt."
"In those days with pain, wonderful. I sometimes examine my behavior when I get angry with some people and myself."

9. What can the Ministry do to improve the way you see, think, or feel about yourself?
"The ministry can be supportive and encouraging to me. Some classes wouldn't hurt."
"Help me to understand the "don't care" attitude of my fellow man. Provide guidelines to help others acknowledge the fact that materials things are not everything."

"I need to believe in what the ministry is teaching and allow God to have His way with my life."

"I would feel much better about myself and the way I see and think about myself if I could do something to help the young people at the church. I would like to help the young people, mostly my family members."

"I think the preacher should preach a sermon that I can live by."

"Identify specific positive attributes or actions and acknowledge them. When I'm admired or appreciated, it motivates me to 'keep on keeping on.' It reinforces the concept that 'I am special and important. A basic need.'"

"Keep me focused on the good aspects of life with examples from the Word and other people's experience with the journey through life."

"Keep teaching the Word, always to keep us focused."

"Good question."

"Continue encouragement and support."

"It can keep on encouraging me to be prayerful and to read God's word. Tell me in a loving and caring way when I am wrong, encourage me to talk more about my personal problems and not to be ashamed of making mistakes."

"Continue to pray for me, I mean the church, since you don't know who I am."

CPSIA information can be obtained at www.ICGtesting.com
Printed in the USA
LVOW10*1110271115

464383LV00004B/10/P